D1601482

J. H. Tilden, M.D.

TOXEMIA
EXPLAINED

By Dr. Tilden

...

TOXEMIA EXPLAINED

·

DR. TILDEN'S COOK BOOK

·

CHILDREN, THEIR HEALTH
AND HAPPINESS

·

DR. TILDEN'S HEALTH
REVIEW & CRITIQUE
A Monthly Magazine

TOXEMIA EXPLAINED

REVISED EDITION

THE TRUE INTERPRETATION
OF THE CAUSE OF DISEASE

HOW TO CURE IS AN OBVIOUS
SEQUENCE

AN ANTIDOTE
TO FEAR, FRENZY
AND THE POPULAR
MAD CHASING AFTER
SO-CALLED CURES

By J. H. TILDEN, M. D.

1,500 Impressions

1960

3,000   1965

3,000   1972

3,000   1980

1,000   1981

Republished 1960

Health Research
P. O. Box 850
Pomeroy, WA 99347
www.healthresearchbooks.com

DEDICATION

WHAT more can be asked by any doctor or layman than a philosophy of the cause of disease that gives a perfect understanding of all the so-called diseases?

To know cause supplies even the layman with a dependable knowledge of how to avoid building disease, and how to cure. When people know how to avoid disease they know an immunization that immunizes rationally.

Dependable knowledge of what disease really is and its cause is man's salvation; and when it can be had with no more effort than that required to read carefully and understandingly Toxemia Explained, there is little excuse for anyone, lay or professional, to live in ignorance of it.

Knowledge is power. Knowledge of how to have health gives greatest power.

Few people know anything about the cause of disease. To them this book is dedicated and the freedom from medical superstition it will bring them.

J. H. TILDEN.

Publisher's Preface

Dr. John H. Tilden, the son of a physician, was born in Van Burenburg, Illinois, on January 21, 1851. He received his medical education at the Eclectic Medical Institute, Cincinnati, Ohio, a medical school founded in 1830 as a protest against the allopathic and homeopathic schools of medicine of that time. He was graduated in 1872, with the degree of doctor of medicine. From the best information we can obtain, his father was a Dr. Joseph G. Tilden, who came from Vermont in 1837 to Kentucky, in which State he married.

Dr. John H. Tilden started the practice of medicine at Nokomis, Illinois, then for a year at St. Louis, Missouri, and then at Litchfield, Illinois, until 1890, when he moved to Denver, Colorado. In Denver he located in the downtown business section, in an office with other doctors. Later he established a sanitarium in an outer section of the city. This sanitarium and school he conducted until 1924, when he sold the Institution, for about half of what he had plowed back into its development, to a Dr. Arthur Voss, of Cincinnati, Ohio, intending to devote himself to writing and lecturing. However, he soon became discontented without his school and after a period he bought two residences on Pennsylvania Avenue, in Denver, united them into one and opened a new sanitarium and school, having to borrow from a friend a part of the money with which to make the purchases. This probably was in 1926. This school continued until the Doctor's death, on September 1, 1940.

It was during the early years of his practice in Illinois, that Dr. Tilden began to question the use of medicine to cure illness. His extensive reading, especially of medical studies from European medical schools, and his own thinking, led him to the conclusion that there should be some way to live so as not to build disease, and in this period his thoughts on toxemia began to formulate and materially develop. From the beginning of his practice in Denver, the Doctor used no medicine but practiced his theory of clearing the body of toxic poison and then allowing nature to make the cure, teaching his patients how to live so as not to create a toxic condition and to retain a healthy body free of disease. An uncompromising realist and a strict disciplinarian, the Doctor wasted no time on those who would not relinquish degenerating habits, but to his patients and disciples he was both friend and mentor.

In 1900 he began the publication of a monthly magazine called "The Stuffed Club," which continued until 1915, when he changed the name to "The Philosophy of Health," and in 1926 the name was changed to "Health Review and Critique." His writing for his publication was almost entirely done in the early morning hours, from three until seven. The purpose of the publication was not to make money but to spread knowledge of the Doctor's teachings. In time it attained a wide circulation, not only in this country but also abroad, even in Australia, but it never produced revenue, for the Doctor refused to make it an advertising medium, as often urged to do by advertising firms. As his death revealed, after sixty-eight years of practice, the Doctor had accumulated only an exceedingly modest estate. His life was pre-eminently one of self-sacrifice and of devotion to service, searching after truth, with an indomitable will and with an intense fortitude to adhere to the truth when discovered. In his day the Doctor's thoughts received no support from the established medical profession but brought the strongest of opposition and condemnation.

Frederic N. Gilbert

Table of Contents

𝒫REFACE

FROM time immemorial, man has looked for a savior; and, when not looking for a savior, he is looking for a cure. He believes in paternalism. He is looking to get something for nothing, not knowing that the highest price we ever pay for anything is to have it given to us.

Instead of accepting salvation, it is better to deserve it. Instead of buying, begging, or stealing a cure, it is better to stop building disease. Disease is of man's own building, and one worse thing than the stupidity of buying a cure is to remain so ignorant as to believe in cures.

The false theories of salvation and cures have built man into a mental mendicant, when he should be the arbiter of his own salvation, and certainly his own doctor, instead of being a slave to a profession that has neither worked out its own salvation from disease nor discovered a single cure in all the age-long period of man's existence on earth.

We hear of diet cures, dietitians, balanced rations, meat diets, vegetable diets, and other diets —chemically prepared foods of all kinds. The reading public is bewildered with hundreds of health magazines and thousands of health ideas. There are thousands writing on health who would not recognize it if they should meet it on the street. Fanaticism, bigotry, stupidity, and commercialism are the principal elements in the dietetic complex that is now belaboring the public.

Cures are what the people want, and cures are what doctors and cultists affect to make; but at most only relief is given.

The periodicity which characterizes all functional derangements of the body lends color to the claims of cure-mongers that their remedy has cured their patients, when the truth is that the so-called disease "ran its course." The truth is that the so-called disease was a toxemic crisis, and when the toxin was eliminated below the toleration point, the sickness passed—automatically health returned. But the disease was not cured; for the cause (enervating habits) is continued, toxin still accumulates, and in due course of time another crisis appears. Unless the cause of Toxemia is discovered and removed, crises will recur until functional derangements will give way to organic disease.

The entire profession is engaged in doctoring crises of Toxemia—curing (?) and curing (?) until overtaken with chronic disease of whatever organ was the seat of the toxin crisis.

THERE ARE NO CURES

Nature returns to normal when enervating habits are given up. There are no cures in the sense generally understood. If one has a tobacco

heart, what is the remedy? Stop the use of tobacco, of course. If the heart is worn out from
shock, as we see it among gamblers, or among men
who are plunging in the stock market, what will
cure? Drugs? No! Removing the cause.

Every so-called disease is built within the mind
and body by enervating habits. The food and
dietetic insanity that constitutes the headliner on
the medical stage just now is causing the people
to demand a diet that will cure them of their peculiar maladies. The idea prevails that some peculiar
diet will cure rheumatism or any other disease.
Diet or food *will not cure any disease.*

A fast, rest in bed, and the giving-up of enervating habits, mental and physical, will allow nature to eliminate the accumulated toxin; then, if
enervating habits are given up, and rational living
habits adopted, health will come back to stay, if
the one CURED will "stay put." This applies to
any so-called disease. Yes, it fits your disease—
you who write to find out if the Tilden system of
cure applies to your case. Yes; cannot you realize
that law and order pervades the universe? And
it is the same from nebula to stone, from stone to
plant, from plant to animal, from animal to man,
from man to mind, and from mind to super-mind
—God. To use a blanket expression: Law and
order pervades the universe, the same yesterday,
today and forever, and is the same from star-dust
to mind—from electron to mind. Toxemia explains how the universal law operates in health

and disease. One disease is the same as another; one man the same as another; one flower the same as another; the carbon in bread, sugar, coal, and the diamond is the same. Yes, one disease can be cured (?) the same as another, unless the organ acted on by toxemic crisis is destroyed.

For example: If wrong eating is persisted in, the acid fermentation first irritates the mucous membrane of the stomach; the irritation becomes inflammation, then ulceration, then thickening and hardening, which ends in cancer at last. The medical world is struggling to find the cause of cancer. It is the distal end of an inflammatory process whose proximal beginning may be any irritation. The end is degeneration from a lack of oxygen and nutriment, and, in degenerating, the septic material enters the circulation, setting up chronic septic poisoning called cancer cachexia.

Disease is a common expression of universal enervation. And understanding of physiology and pathology necessitates a firm grip on evolution as expressed in biology; or reasoning will go astray occasionally.

Modern cures and immunization are vanity and vexation; they are founded on the foolish principle of reasoning from effect, which is disease, to cause. The organ which is suffering from many crises of Toxemia is discovered—it may be ulcer of the stomach, then the ulcer is cut out; it may be gallstone, then the stone is cut out; it may be fibroid tumor of the womb, then the tumor or womb is cut out. The same may be said of other effects—the medical armament is turned loose on a lot of effects. This is accepted by the public mind as efficient treatment of disease, when in fact it is a stupid removal of effects. And that is not the worst of such blundering. The operators have not the slightest idea of the cause of the effects they so skillfully remove.

In other derangements the same lack of knowledge of cause prevails. In the treatment of deficiency diseases, the lacking element is supplied from the laboratory; but nothing is done in the line of restoring the organ to normality. Why? Because medical science has not discovered why organs fail to function properly; and until this discovery is made, scientific blundering will continue.

THE WORLD NEEDS THE SCIENCE OF SURGERY

If mutilation (unnecessary surgery) is required in nine hundred and ninety-nine cases to perfect the skill required in the thousandth case, the question of the need of high-class surgery must be answered by the mutilated or vandalized class.

Is war necessary? What would be the answer of the 7,485,000 who were killed in the late World War, if the question were submitted to them? Estimate $5,000 as the man-power loss for each man; then the world lost $37,425,000,000 in this one item alone. Surgery costs the world, in vandalizing the bodies of men, women, and children, as much every year. Is it worth that much for all the real good it does? Why is so much surgery thought to be necessary? Because of the ignorance of the people, egged on by a science-mad or selfish profession. It is more spectacular to operate than to teach people how to live to avoid chronic disease and operations.

ARE PALLIATIVES EVER NECESSARY?

It is doubtful if the palliation which doctors and cultists give is worth the disadvantage that the sick habit taught the patients by their doctor brings them.

The drug habit taught the thousands certainly overbalances any relief given. Drugs to relieve pain are never necessary. Twenty-five years in which I used drugs, and twenty-eight in which I have not used drugs, should make my belief, that drugs are unnecessary and in most cases injurious, worth something to those who care to know the truth.

YES, VENEREAL DISEASES CAN BE CURED WITHOUT DRUGS

I make no exception of syphilis, and stand ready to demonstrate the truth of what I say at any time and anywhere to a committee of doctors.

Nature cures—nature can eliminate syphilis, or any type of infection, if all enervating habits are given up and a rational mode of living adopted.

STIMULANTS ARE SUBTILELY UNDERMINING

So insidious in their action are all stimulants that the unwary are surprised by finding themselves more or less slaves to them when they are not conscious of using them to excess.

The coffee headache is an example. A time comes when it is not convenient to get the usual breakfast cup. A dullness or languid feeling appears three or four hours after breakfast, that cannot be accounted for until some friend suggests that perhaps it is due to missing the coffee; but the victim is not convinced until he proves it true by trying it out several times. Some develop a headache, and still others are troubled with gaping or yawning and a feeling of oppression, due to heart enervation brought on from the use of coffee.

At first stimulants gently remove awareness— remove tire and actuate the mind and body. It should be obvious to reasoning minds that borrowed activity must be paid for sooner or later.

Using nerve-energy in excess of normal production brings on enervation. Few people waste nerve-energy in one way only. Food is a stimulant. Overeating is overstimulating. Add to this excess one or two other stimulants—coffee or tobacco—excessive venery, overwork and worry, and one subject to that amount of drain of nerve-energy will become decidedly enervated. Elimination falls far short of requirements; consequently toxin accumulates in the blood. This adds a pronounced auto-toxin stimulation to the coming from overstimulating habits, and completes a vicious circle. This complex stands for a disease-producing Toxemia, which will be permanent except as toxin crises—so-called acute diseases—lower the amount of toxin, again to accumulate and continue until the habits that keep the body enervated are controlled. Perfect health cannot be established until all enervating habits have been eliminated.

DEFINITION of Toxemia and crises of Toxemia:—In the process of tissue building—metabolism—there is cell building—anabolism — and cell destruction — catabolism. The broken down tissue is toxic and in health—when nerve energy is normal it is eliminated from the blood as fast as evolved. When nerve energy is dissipated from any cause—physical or mental excitement or bad habits—the body becomes enervated, when enervated elimination is checked causing a retention of toxin in the blood or Toxemia. This accumulation of toxin when once established will continue until nerve energy is restored by removing the causes. So-called disease is nature's effort at eliminating the toxin from the blood. All so-called diseases are crises of Toxemia.

Introduction to Toxemia

THE medical world has built an infinite literature without any (except erroneous and vacillating) ideas of cause. Medicine is rich in science, but now, as well as in all past time, it suffers from a dearth of practical ideas. The average doctor is often educated out of all the common-sense he was born with. This, however, is not his fault. It is the fault of the system. He is an educated automaton. He has facts—scientific facts galore—without ideas. Ford has mechanical facts—not more, perhaps, than thousands of other mechanics, but he joined them to an idea which made him a multimillionaire. Millions have facts, but no ideas. Thousands of doctors have all the scientific data needed, but they have not harnessed their science to common-sense and philosophy.

Without a clear conception of cause, cure must remain the sphinx that it is.

The late Sir James Mackenzie—while living, the greatest clinician in the world—declared: "In medical research the object is mainly the prevention and cure of disease." If cause is not known, how is prevention or cure possible—as, for example, by producing a mild form of smallpox or other so-called disease by poisoning a healthy person by introducing into his body the pathological products of said disease? Certainly only pathological thinking can arrive at such conclusions. Vaccines and autogenous remedies are made from the products of disease, and the idea that disease can be made to cure itself is an end-product of pathological thinking. This statement is not so incongruous after we consider the fact that all search and research work to find cause by medical scientists has been made in dead and dying people. As ridiculous as it may appear, medical science has gone, and is still going, to the dead and dying to find cause.

If prevention and cure mean producing disease, surely prevention and cure are not desirable. If prevention can be accomplished, then cures will not be needed.

At the time of his death, Mackenzie was laboring to discover prevention. A more worthy work can not be imagined. But the tragedy of his life was that he died from a preventable disease; and he could have cured the disease that killed him if his conception of cause had been in line with the Truth of Toxemia—the primary cause of all disease.

In spite of Mackenzie's ambition to put the profession in possession of truth concerning prevention and cure, he died without a correct idea of even in what direction to look for this desirable knowledge, as evidenced by such statements as: "Our problems being the prevention of disease, we require a complete knowledge of disease in all its aspects before we can take steps to prevent its occurrence." There is the crux of the whole subject. It is not disease; it is cause "in all its aspects" that we need to know before we can take steps to prevent "disease." Mackenzie stated the following concerning diagnosis:

But it appears to be unlikely that in the present state of medicine there would be any great dissimilarity in the proportions of diagnosed and undiagnosed cases in many series of investigation such as we have made. The proportion depends, not on the skill or training of individual practitioners, but on the unsatisfactory state of all medical knowledge. The similarity of the statistical records from the institute and from private practice goes far to support this view. In spite of the additional time given at the institute to the examination of cases which are undiagnosable in general practice, and the assistance given by the special departments—clinical groups—in their investigation, they remain profoundly obscure, although we know that it is from among them that there will gradually emerge the cases of advanced organic disease and the end-results which form so large a proportion of the inmates of hospital wards. And the tragedy is that many of them suffer from no serious disabilities, and might, but for our ignorance, be checked on their downward course.

Isn't this about as sharp a criticism of medical inefficiency as Tilden has ever made?

This brings vividly to mind the statement, made only a short time ago, by Dr. Cabot, of Boston, that he himself was mistaken in his diagnoses about fifty per cent of the time—that he had proved it by post-mortems. Such a statement as this, coming from a man of his standing, means much. To me it means that diagnosis is a meaningless term; for, as used, it means discovering what pathological effects—what changes—have been brought about by an undiscovered cause. Diagnosis means, in a few words, discovering effects which, when found, throw no light whatever on cause.

Again I quote Mackenzie: "The knowledge of disease is so incomplete that we do not yet even know what steps should be taken to advance our knowledge." This being true, there is little excuse for laws to shut out or prevent cults from practicing less harmful palliations. How many reputable physicians have the honesty of Sir James Mackenzie?

In spite of Mackenzie's high and worthy ambitions, he could not get away from the profession's stereotyped thinking. The early symptoms of disease he declared held the secret of their cause, and he believed an intense study of them would give the facts. But functional derangements are of the same nature and from the same universal cause that ends in all organic so-called diseases. All so-called diseases are, from beginning to end, the same evolutionary process.

The study of pathology—the study of disease—has engaged the best minds in the profession always, and it surely appears that the last word must have been spoken on the subject; but the great Englishman believed, as all research workers believe, that a more intense and minute study of the early symptoms of disease will reveal the cause. There is, however, one great reason why it cannot, and that is that all symptom-complexes—diseases—from their initiation to their ending, are effects, and the most intense study of any phase or stage of their progress will not throw any light on the cause.

Cause is constant, ever present, and always the same. Only effects, and the object on which cause acts, change, and the change is most inconstant. To illustrate: A catarrh of the stomach presents first irritation, then inflammation, then ulceration, and finally induration and cancer. Not all cases run true to form; only a small percentage evolve to ulcer, and fewer still reach the cancer stage. More exit by way of acute food-poisoning or acute indigestion than by chronic diseases.

In the early stages of this evolution there are all kinds of discomforts: more or less attacks of indigestion, frequent attacks of gastritis—sick stomach and vomiting. No two cases are alike. Nervous people suffer most, and some present all kinds of nervous symptoms—insomnia, headaches, etc. Women have painful menstruation and hysterical symptoms—some are morose and others have epilepsy. As the more chronic symptoms appear, those of the lymphatic temperament do not suffer so much. As the disease progresses, a few become pallid and develop pernicious anemia, due to gastric or intestinal ulceration and putrid protein infection; in others the first appearance of ulcer is manifested by a severe hemorrhage; others have a cachexia and a retention of food in the stomach, which is vomited every two or three days, caused by a partial closing of the pylorus. These are usually malignant cases.

To look upon any of these symptom-complexes as a distinct disease, requiring a distinct treatment, is to fall into the diagnostic maze that now bewilders the profession and renders treatment chaotic.

It should be known to all discerning physicians that the earliest stage of organic disease is purely functional, evanescent, and never autogenerated, so far as the affected organ is concerned, but is invariably due to an extraneous irritation (stimulation, if you please), augmented by Toxemia when the irritation is not continuous, and toxin is eliminated as fast as developed, to the toleration point, normal functioning is resumed between the intervals of irritation and toxin excess.

For example: a simple coryza (running at the nose—cold in the head), gastritis, or colonitis. At first these colds, catarrhs, or inflammations are periodic and functional; but, as the exciting cause or causes—local irritation and Toxemia—become more intense and continuous, the mucous membranes of these organs take on organic changes, which are given various names, such as irritation, inflammation, ulceration, and cancer. The pathology (organic change) may be studied until doomsday without throwing any light on the cause; for from the first irritation to the extreme ending—cachexia—which may be given the blanket term of tuberculosis, syphilis, or cancer, the whole pathologic panorama is one continuous evolution of intensifying effects.

Germs and other so-called causes may be discovered in the course of pathological development, but they are accidental, coincidental, or at most auxiliary—or, to use the vernacular of law, *obiter dicta.*

The proper way to study disease is to study health and every influence favorable or not to its continuance. Disease is perverted health. Any influence that lowers nerve-energy becomes disease-producing. Disease cannot be its own cause; neither can it be its own cure, and certainly not its own prevention.

After years of wandering in the jungle of medical diagnosis—the usual guesswork of cause and effect, and the worse-than-guesswork of treatment —and becoming more confounded all the time, I resolved either to quit the profession or to find the cause of disease. To do this, it was necessary to exile myself from doctors and medical conventions; for I could not think for myself while listening to the babblings of babeldom. I took the advice found in Matt. 6:6. According to prevailing opinion, unless a doctor spends much time in medical societies and in the society of other doctors, takes postgraduate work, travels, etc., he cannot keep abreast of advancement.

This opinion would be true if the sciences of medicine were fitted to a truthful etiology (efficient cause) of disease. But, since they are founded on no cause, or at most speculative and spectacular causes, as unstable as the sands of the sea, the doctor who cannot brook the bewilderment of vacillation is compelled to hide away from the voices of mistaken pedants and knowing blatherskites until stabilized. By that time ostracism will have overtaken him, and his fate, metaphorically speaking, will be that of the son of Zacharias.

An honest search after truth too often, if not always, leads to the rack, stake, cross, or the blessed privilege of recanting; but the victim, by this time, decides as did the divine Jew: "Not my will, but thine, be done;" or, as Patrick Henry declared: "Give me liberty or give me death!" The dying words of another great Irishman is the wish, no doubt, of every lover of freedom and truth:

That no man write my epitaph; for, as no man who knows my motive dares now vindicate them, let not prejudice or ignorance asperse them. Let them and me rest in peace, and my tomb remain uninscribed, and my memory in oblivion, until other times and other men can do justice to my character. When my country takes her place among the nations of the earth, then, and not until then, let my epitaph be written. (Emmet).

The truth is larger than any man, and, until it is established, the memory of its advocate is not important. In the last analysis, is not the truth the only immortality? Man is an incident. If he discovers a truth, it benefits all who accept it. Truth too often must pray to be delivered from its friends.

I must acknowledge that I have not been very courteous to indifferent convention; and the truth I have discovered has suffered thereby. It has always appeared to me that the attention of fallacy-mongers cannot be attracted except by the use of a club or shillalah; and possibly my style of presenting my facts has caused too great a shock, and the desired effect has been lost in the reaction.

That I have discovered the true cause of disease cannot be successfully disputed. This being true, my earnestness in presenting this great truth is justifiable.

When I think back over my life, and remember the struggle I had with myself in supplanting my old beliefs with the new—the thousands of times I have suspected my own sanity—I then cannot be surprised at the opposition I have met and am meeting.

My discovery of the truth that Toxemia is the cause of all so-called diseases came about slowly, step by step, with many dangerous skids.

At first I believed that enervation must be the general cause of disease; then I decided that simple enervation is not disease, that disease must be

due to poison, and that poison, to be the general cause of disease, must be autogenerated; and if disease is due to an autogenerated poison, what is the cause of that autogeneration? I dallied long in endeavoring to trace disease back to poison taken into the system, such as food eaten after putrescence had begun, or from poisoning due to the development of putrescence after ingestion. In time I decided that poisoning per se is not disease. I observed where poisoning did not kill; some cases reacted and were soon in full health, while others remained in a state of semi-invalidism. I found the same thing true of injuries and mental shock. It took a long time to develop the thought that a poisoned or injured body, when not overwhelmed by Toxemia, would speedily return to the normal; and when it did not, there was a sick habit—a derangement of some kind—that required some such contingency to bring it within sense-perception.

To illustrate: An injury to a joint is often complicated with rheumatism; the rheumatism previous to the injury was potentially in the blood.

Just what change had taken place in the organism which, under stress of injury or shock of any kind, would cause a reaction with fever I could not understand until the Toxemic Theory suggested itself to my mind, after which the cause of disease unfolded before me in an easy and natural manner. And now the theory is a proved fact.

After years of perplexing thought and "watchful waiting," I learned that all disease, of whatever nature, was of slow development; that without systemic preparation even so-called acute systemic diseases could not manifest.

In a few words: Without Toxemia there can be no disease. I knew that the waste-product of metabolism was toxic, and that the only reason why we were not poisoned by it was because it was removed from the organism as fast as produced. Then I decided that the toxin was retained in the blood, when there was a checking of elimination. Then the cause of the checking had to be determined. In time I thought out the cause. I knew that, when we had a normal nerve-energy, organic functioning was normal. Then came the thought that enervation caused a checking of elimination. Eureka! The cause of all so-called diseases is found! Enervation checks elimination of the waste-products of metabolism. Retention of metabolic toxin—the first and only cause of disease!

Those who would be freed from the bondage of medical superstition should study "Toxemia Explained."

Toxemia Explained

NO ONE on the outside of the medical profession knows so well as doctors themselves the great need of more knowledge of what disease really is. Never in the history of so-called medical science has there been so much research work done as in the past decade; but with every new discovery there follows very closely on its heels the stark and stalking nemesis that chills the honest and earnest research labor to the bone —the inevitable word *Failure*. Why inevitable? Because, back in the beginning of man's reasoning on the subject of his discomforts, his pains, and his sicknesses, he made the monstrous mistake that something outside of himself—outside of his own volition—had wished him harm. Man being a religious animal, he early thought he had in some manner offended one of his many deities. The history of how man evolved the idea of disease being an entity is too long to do more than allude to it in a book of this kind. Any of the old mythologies may be referred to by those who are curious enough to look the matter up. That man is still saturated with centuries of mythological inheritance was brought out vividly when the germ theory was introduced. It answered the instinctive call for demoniacal possession! At last man's search for the demon—the author of all his woes —had been discovered, and a satisfactory apology could be made to his conscience for all his apparent shortcomings. However, fifty years of vicarious atonement for man's sins by the demon germ are waning, and reason be praised if the microbe is the last excuse that man can make for his sins of omission and commission before the throne of his own reason!

Medical science is founded on a false premise— namely, that disease is caused by extraneous influences, and that drugs are something that cures or palliates discomfort. The term "medical" means pertaining to medicine or the practice of medicine. Anything used in a remedial way carries the idea of curing, healing, correcting, or affording relief; and this doctoring is all done without any clear understanding of cause.

The words "medical," "medicine," "disease," and "cure" have become concrete in our understanding, and shape our thoughts and beliefs. And so arbitrary are these beliefs that new schools and cults are forced to the conventional understanding. They may declare that an impinged nerve is the cause of any pathology. But they do not trouble themselves to find why one impinged nerve creates a pathology and another does not.

The psychologist does not trouble himself to explain why worry in one subject causes disease and in another it does not; why hope in one subject cures and in another it does not; why negation does not always cure; why faith does not always cure; begging the question by declaring that there was not faith enough, etc. No fool is a bigger fool than the fool who fools himself.

Why should not all new schools of thought be found harking back to their mother-thought—I say, why not? So long as the idea that disease is a reality, an individuality, an entity, is firmly fixed in the mind, even those in research work will be controlled and directed in their labors by the conventional understanding. That is why every wonderful discovery soon proves a mistaken belief.

There is no hope that medical science will ever be a science; for the whole structure is built around the idea that there is an object—disease—that can be cured when the right drug—remedy, cure—is found.

It is my intention to portray the common, every-day foibles of scientific medicine so that the people may see the absurdities concerning disease and cure in which they are and have been hoodwinked into believing by the blare of science. Then I shall describe the only worked-out rational explanation of the cause of so-called diseases, hoping, by contrasting the old and new, to start a few to thinking and building new brain-cells, which in time may supersede the old and conventional.

Until Toxemia was discovered and elaborated

by myself into a medical philosophy there was no real medical philosophy. The cause and cure of disease is and has been a medley of guesswork and speculation which has confounded the best and most industrious medical minds in every generation.

Today, as never before, the brightest minds in the profession are delving into research work, endeavoring to find the efficient cause of disease. But they are doomed to disappointment; for they fail at their beginning. Why? Because all the work that has ever been done in searching for cause has been along the line of critical study and examination of effects; and certainly reasoning minds cannot believe that an effect can be its own cause. No one believes in spontaneous generation. The remnant of this belief was annihilated by Pasteur's discovery of germs as the cause of fermentation—a discovery so profound that it created a frenzy in the medical world; and, as in every epidemic of frenzy, mental poise was lost. The importance of the germ as a primary or efficient cause of disease was accepted *nolens volens*, willy nilly. Everyone was swept off his feet. As in all sudden gushes in change of belief, it was dangerous not to agree with the mob spirit; hence opposing or conservative voices were suppressed or ostracized.

The germ frenzy was fierce for two or three decades; but now it is a thing of the past and will soon be, if it is not now, a dead letter.

Cause of disease is being looked for everywhere, and no less a personage than the late Sir James Mackenzie, in "Reports of the St. Andrews Institute for Clinical Research," Volume I, declared: "The knowledge of disease is so incomplete that we do not yet even know what steps should be taken to advance our knowledge." At another time he wrote: "Disease is made manifest to us only by the symptoms which it produces; the first object in the examination of a patient is the detection of symptoms, and therefore the symptoms of disease form one of the main objects of our study."

THE VALUE OF SYMPTOMATOLOGY

Sir James, when living, was probably the greatest clinician of the English-speaking world; yet he had not outlived the medical superstition that disease is a positive entity, and that the way to find disease is to trace symptoms to their source. But if a symptom is traced to its source, what of it? A pain is traced to its source, and we find that it comes from the head. The head does not cause the pain. Then we find that there are symptoms of hyperemia—too much blood in the head. The pressure from too much blood in the head causes the pain. Then pressure must be the disease? No. Then too much blood is the disease—hyperemia? Certainly; too much blood in the head has a cause. What is it that causes congestion? We find that pain is a symptom. Pressure causes pain; it, too, is a symptom. Too much blood in the head causes pressure; it also is a symptom. Pain, pressure, hyperemia are, all three, symptoms. In time the walls of the blood-vessels weaken, and the pressure ruptures one of the vessels. Hemorrhage into the brain causes death from apoplexy. Is the ruptured blood-vessel the disease? No. Is hemorrhage into the brain the disease? No; it is a symptom. Is death from hemorrhage the disease?

If the hemorrhage is not severe enough to cause death, but does produce some form of paralysis—and there can be many kinds—is paralysis a disease? Haven't we been traveling along a chain of symptoms from headache to paralysis? We have not found anything to which all these symptoms point as disease; and, according to the requirements of Sir James Mackenzie, disease is made manifest to us only by symptoms. Here we have a chain of symptoms beginning with pain, ending in hemorrhage and death or paralysis, without giving us any indication whatever of cause as understood. Any other chain, namely, stomach symptoms, ending in pyloric cancer, will not give any more indication of disease at the various stages than the foregoing illustration.

The first symptom we have of any chain of symptoms is discomfort or pain. In any stomach derangement we have pain, more or less aggravated by food. Catarrh follows, or more often precedes, it—or what we call inflammation or gastritis. Gastritis continues, with a thickening of the mucous membrane. A time comes when there is ulceration. This will be called a disease, and is recognized as ulcer of the stomach; but it is only a continuation of the primary symptom of catarrh and pain. The ulcer is removed, but the symptom of inflammation and pain continues, and other ulcers will follow. This state eventually merges into induration or hardening of the pyloric orifice of the stomach. When this develops, there is more or less obstruction to the outlet causing occasional vomiting, and, on thorough examination, cancer is found.

If we analyze the symptoms from the first pain and catarrh in the stomach, we shall find the chain of symptoms running along. The first symptom to be noticed is pain. On examination, we find a catarrhal condition of the stomach; and this catarrhal condition is not a disease—it is a symptom. Catarrhal inflammation continues, with the thickening of the mucous membrane, which finally ends in ulceration. Ulceration is not the disease; it is only a continuation of the inflammatory symptom. If the ulcer is removed, it does not remove the disease; it only removes a symptom. These symptoms continue until there is a thickening and induration of the pyloris, which is called cancer. And yet we have not discovered anything but symptoms from beginning to end.

By removing the cancer, the question of what the disease is has not been answered. Cancer being the end-symptom, it cannot be the cause of the first symptom.

Any other so-called disease can be worked out in the same way. Pain and catarrh are the first symptoms, as a rule, that call a physician's or a patient's attention to anything being wrong; and pain and catarrh are not the disease. When the cause of the pain is found, it too will be found a symptom and not a disease. And this will be true to the end.

It is no wonder that diagnosticians become perplexed in their search after disease, because they have confounded symptoms and disease. The fact of the matter is, it is impossible to put the finger on any ending of a chain of symptoms and say: "This is the disease." In the beginning of this analysis we showed that headache, or pain in the head, is not a disease; and when we had finished we found that hemorrhage or apoplexy is not a disease—it is only a continuation of the primary symptoms.

"Disease is made manifest to us only by symptoms which it produces." This statement tacitly infers that there are diseases and symptoms, and that through symptoms we may find disease. When we undertake to trace symptoms to disease, we are in the dilemma of a mountain-climber who, on reaching the top of one mountain, finds other peaks, and higher ones, farther on and on.

That Mackenzie had been baffled in his search

for fixed disease is indicated in the following, which I quote from the reports mentioned before:

Many diseases are considered to be of a dangerous nature, and many attempts are made to combat the danger, with, however, no perception of its nature. This is particularly the case with epidemic diseases, such as measles, influenza, scarlet fever, and diphtheria. As a consequence, proposals have at different times been put forward to treat individuals who suffer from these diseases upon some general plan, without consideration of the peculiarities of the individual case—and thus we get that rule-of-thumb treatment which is shown in the indiscriminate use of a serum or vaccine.

During influenza epidemics there is always a cry for a universal method of treatment, and attempts are made to meet this cry in the shape of so-called specifics and vaccines.

When a great authority declares that dangerous diseases are combated without any perception of their nature—and that, too, in spite of the germ theory—it should be obvious to thinking minds that the germ theory has been weighed and found wanting. Yet, when something must be done, and nothing better has been discovered, "serums and vaccines may be used indiscriminately."

That the "rule of thumb" is the rule governing all thinking concerning symptoms, diseases, their cause and treatment, is so obvious that anyone possessing a reasoning mind, not camouflaged by scientific buncombe, should read as he runs.

Medicine rests on a sound scientific foundation. Anatomy, physiology, biology, chemistry, and all collateral sciences that have a bearing on the science of man, are advanced to great perfection. But the so-called sciences of symptomatology, disease, diagnosis, etiology, and the treatment of disease go back to superstition for their foundation. We see the incongruity of jumbling real science with delusion and superstition. Disease is believed to be an entity; and this idea is necessarily followed by another as absurd—namely, cure. Around these two old assumptions has grown an infinite literature that confounds its builders.

TRUTH—AS FAMOUS MEN SEE IT

When a man's knowledge is not in order, the more of it he has, the greater will be his confusion.—(Herbert Spencer.)

Confusion worse confounded is the only explanation that can be given of the theory and practice of medicine. Of course, it is hoary with age, and is one of the learned professions. With much just pride can the rank and file point to its aristocracy —its long list of famous dead as well as living physicians? What has made most of them famous? The same that has made others famous in and out of the professions—namely, personal worth and education. Franklin was not a doctor; yet he was as great as any doctor, and could use his gray matter in advising the sick as well as those not sick. He appeared to have a sense-perception for truth; and I would say that his discrimination is the leading, if not the distinguishing, trait that has divided, and always will divide, the really great from the mediocre majority. They are the leaven that leaveneth the whole herd of humanity—the quality of character that could not be found in all Sodom and Gomorrah.

There was another discriminating mind in the eighteenth century—another Benjamin, who also was a signer of the Declaration of Independence—Benjamin Rush, a physician, a luminary that brought distinction to medical science. He was larger than his profession. He left seeds of thought which, if acted upon by the profession, would have organized medical thought and prevented the present-day confusion. He left on record such golden nuggets as:

Much mischief has been done by the nosological arrangement of diseases. . . . Disease is as much a unit as fever. . . . Its different seats and degrees should no more be multiplied into different diseases than the numerous and different effects of heat and light upon our globe should be multiplied into a plurality of suns.

The whole materia medica is infected with the baneful consequences of the nomenclature of disease; for every article in it is pointed only against their names. . . . By the rejection of the artificial arrangement of diseases, a revolution must follow in medicine. . . . The road to knowledge in medicine by this means will likewise be shortened; so that a young man will be able to qualify himself to practice physic at a much less expense of time and labor than formerly, as a child would learn to read and write by the help of the Roman alphabet, instead of Chinese characters.

Science has much to deplore from the multiplication

of diseases. It is as repugnant to truth in medicine as polytheism is to truth in religion. The physician who considers every different affection of the different parts of the same system as distinct diseases, when they arise from one cause, resembles the Indian or African savage who considers water, dew, ice, frost, and snow as distinct essences; while the physician who considers the morbid affections of every part of the body, however diversified they may be in their form or degrees, as derived from one cause, resembles the philosopher who considers dew, ice, frost, and snow as different modifications of water, and as derived simply from the absence of heat.

Humanity has likewise much to deplore from this paganism in medicine. The sword will probably be sheathed forever, as an instrument of death, before physicians will cease to add to the mortality of mankind by prescribing for the names of diseases.

There is but one remote cause of disease. . . . These remarks are of extensive application, and, if duly attended to, would deliver us from a mass of error which has been accumulating for ages in medicine; I mean the nomenclature of diseases from their remote causes. It is the most offensive and injurious part of the rubbish of our science.

The physician who can cure one disease by a knowledge of its principles may by the same means cure all the diseases of the human body; for their causes are the same.

There is the same difference between the knowledge of a physician who prescribes for diseases as limited by genera and species, and of one who prescribes under the direction of just principles, that there is between the knowledge we obtain of the nature and extent of the sky, by viewing a few feet of it from the bottom of a well, and viewing from the top of a mountain the whole canopy of heaven.

I would as soon believe that ratafia was intended by the Author of Nature to be the only drink of man, instead of water, as believe that the knowledge of what relates to the health and lives of a whole city, or nation, should be confined to one, and that a small or a privileged, order of men.

From a short review of these facts, reason and humanity awake from their long repose in medicine, and unite in proclaiming that it is time to take the cure of pestilential epidemics out of the hands of physicians, and to place it in the hands of the people.

Dissections daily convince us of our ignorance of the seats of disease, and cause us to blush at our prescriptions. . . . What mischief have we done under the belief of false facts, if I may be allowed the expression, and false theories! We have assisted in multiplying diseases. We have done more—we have increased their mortality.

I shall not pause to beg pardon of the faculty for acknowledging, in this public manner, the weaknesses of our profession. I am pursuing Truth, and while I can keep my eye fixed upon my guide, I am indifferent whither I am led, provided she is my leader.

Oliver W. Holmes, M. D., was a man who gave dignity and respectability to the profession. He was a literary man, and from his beginning to his end, was always larger than his profession. He once said: "I firmly believe that, if the whole materia medica could be sunk to the bottom of the sea, it would be all the better for mankind and all the worse for the fishes." "Breakfast-Table Series" will be read by the intelligent people of the future, who will know nothing of Holmes' fight for women against the dirty hands of herd-doctors and their consequences—puerperal fever.

"Æquanimitas" will keep Osler in the minds of intelligent people when "Osler's Practice of Medicine" will be found only in the shops of bibliomaniacs. Such men as Osler keep the dead weight of mediocre medicine from sinking to oblivion by embellishing medical fallacies with their superb personalities and their literary polish.

Throughout all the ages the finest minds have sensed the truth concerning the cause of disease, and this has bulked large against medical insanities and inanities.

A very striking picture of the medical herd was made by "Anonymous" in his essay on "Medicine" in "Civilization in the United States":

It has been remarked above that one of the chief causes of the unscientific nature of medicine and the antiscientific character of doctors lies in their innate credulity and inability to think independently. This contention is supported by the report on the intelligence of physicians recently published by the National Research Council. They are found by more or less trustworthy psychologic tests to be lowest in intelligence of all the professional men, excepting only dentists and horse-doctors. Dentists and horse-doctors are ten per cent less intelligent. But since the quantitative methods employed certainly carry an experimental error of ten per cent or even higher, it is not certain that the members of the two more humble professions have not equal or even greater intellectual ability. It is significant that engineers head the list in intelligence. In fact, they are rated sixty per cent higher than doctors.

This wide disparity leads to a temptation to interesting psychological probings. Is not the lamentable lack of intelligence of the doctor due to lack of necessity for rigid intellectual discipline? Many conditions conspire to make him an intellectual cheat. Fortunately for us, most diseases are self-limiting. But it is natural for the physician to turn this dispensation of nature to his advantage and to intimate that *he* has cured John Smith, when actually nature has done the trick. On the contrary, should Smith die, the good doctor can assume a pious expression and suggest that, despite his own incredible skill and tremendous effort, it was God's (or nature's) will that John should pass beyond. Now, the engineer is open to no such temptation. He builds a bridge or erects a building, and disaster is sure to follow any misstep in calculation or fault in construction. Should such a calamity occur, he is presently discredited and disappears from view. Thus he is held up to a high mark of intellectual rigor and discipline that is utterly unknown in the world the doctor inhabits.

The critic appears to think that "one of the chief causes of the anti-scientific character of doctors lies in their innate credulity and inability to think independently." I presume he means that the doctors cannot think independently; for if medicine, scientific or unscientific, could think at all, it might have thought itself out of its present-day muddle.

The only thing that saves all physicians from the above indictment is that they are not examined on the cause and treatment of disease. If average physicians pass low on "trustworthy psychological tests," it does not speak very well for the higher education which put so many medical schools out of business a few years ago. But these psychological tests may be fitted to educational standards which are assembled with intelligence left out. Intelligence, like the *cause of disease*, is a force in nature that can be used under the proper environments; but it cannot be monopolized to the exclusion of all mankind. Gladstone in youth was passed upon by the psychological test of his teacher, and pronounced incorrigible; yet at eighty-six he was wielding an ax and translating Virgil.

SCIENTIFIC TESTS

People should not take too seriously to heart verdicts resting on scientific tests, where a very large part of the integral is scientific assumption and presumption. The New York Life Insurance Company turned me down more than fifty years ago.

"Anonymous," whoever he is, writes well, and, as that of an iconoclast, his style is quite fetching. But, to save his bacon, it was well that he criticized from ambush; for he would make an excellent target. From my point of view, I find him as vulnerable as any Standard A type of professional men.

He shows his medical length and breadth when he says: "Of all the dreadful afflictions that plague us, a few may be cured or ameliorated by the administration of remedies." That was said by medical men now one and two hundred years dead, and with no more aplomb than that of the doctors of today in the literary class of our "Anonymous."

"Dreadful afflictions" do not "plague us." If we are plagued by disease, it is of our own building; and all we need to do to get back to comfort and health is to quit building it; then our subconscious self gets busy cleaning house.

"Anonymous" could not have made a statement that would have been more perfectly one hundred per cent fallacy. He says: "A few may be cured." That is a mild statement, coming from one of the ambushed Cæsars of scientific medicine. I presume he means that there is a contingent possibility that a few can be cured. This is false; for "afflictions" or disease cannot be cured. Nature —our subconsciousness—has a full monopoly on the power to cure. Healing is nature's prerogative, and she cannot, if she would, delegate it to doctors or to the academies of medical science.

What a glorious legacy, vouchsafed by the powers that be! What a sad plight humanity would be in if medical commercialism had a monopoly on healing or curing the sick! It does very well, however, as it is vending its camouflage cures of all kinds. But when mankind awakens to a full realization of the truth that for all past time it has been buying a pretense of power that it alone possesses a monopoly, old hoary-headed Æsculapius will be unfrocked and thrown out of business— staff, snake, and all.

"Anonymous," fearing that the statements, "A few may be cured," was too strong, added the modifying phrase "or ameliorated;" which, in medical parlance, means palliated, relieved, etc. This in reality is the whole truth concerning so-called remedies or cures. And when the truth is known that curing, or the power to throw off disease and get well is wholly within the subconscious and is personal, we will know that curing and palliating by the administration of remedies—drugs, serums, vaccines, surgery, feeding to keep up the strength, etc.—are superfluous, meddlesome, and on the order of throwing a monkey-wrench into the machinery.

After criticizing "Anonymous" for what we know, inferentially, that he stands for, we will quote the remainder of what he says concerning the treatment of the "dreadful afflictions that plague us." He further declares:

And an equally small number improved or were abolished by surgical interference. But, in spite of the relatively few diseases to which surgery is beneficial, the number of surgeons that flourished in the land is enormous. The fundamental discoveries of Pasteur, and their brilliant application by Lister, were quickly seized upon in America. The names of Bull, Halstead, Murphy, the brothers Mayo, Cushing, and Finney are to be ranked with those of the best surgeons of any nation. In fact, we may be said to lead the world—to use an apt Americanism—in the production of surgeons [and surgical plants], just as we do in that of automobiles, baby-carriages, and antique furniture.

"A few diseases may be cured or ameliorated." I say, never cured; and amelioration is a form of building disease.

A delicate woman became my patient, after suffering from megrim for twenty-two years and taking more or less palliatives from twenty-two different doctors—a few widely known, one a neurologist of more than national fame; the majority of whom told her that there was no cure, but that, when she changed life, the headaches would cease. This was a "bum" guess; for she declared that her suffering had been greater the past two years, since her menstruation has ceased, than ever before. Just how much the psychological suggestion, made by fifteen or twenty doctors, that she would not get well for a given time, had to do with prolonging her headaches, no one can tell. Drug palliation is always inclined to enervate and build Toxemia. This woman had been relieved by hypodermics of morphine—a fiendish treatment. There should be a law against such malpractice. But the majority never handicap themselves with prohibitory laws.

My prescription was: No more smoking in the home (the husband being an inveterate smoker); stay in bed; fast, take a tub bath and an enema every night until a paroxysm of headache had been missed.

The paroxysms had been coming weekly, beginning on Tuesday and leaving her prostrate until Friday. Orders were given for a hot bath to be given to full relief, even if it required an hour. The patient had only one paroxysm after becoming my patient, and that required three-quarters of an hour in a hot bath to relieve. The husband became very enthusiastic over the fact that his wife had been relieved of her pain for the first time in twenty-two years without drugs. My comment on his outburst of rejoicing was: "Your smoking and the doctor's drugging were responsible for her unnecessary suffering during nearly a quarter of a century."

Drugging pain of any kind checks elimination and prevents the human organism from cleaning house. In this case of megrim, every time an eliminating crisis developed, the doctor slammed the doors of egress shut and barred them with morphine. My prescription reversed the order; it opened all the doors, with the result that she never had another headache after the one that the hot bath relieved. Of course, I tinkered with her eating and other habits afterward. People are never sick who have no bad habits.

About the same time I advised another woman who had suffered weekly from paroxysms of megrim for sixteen years. Like the first case, she had been medicated by many doctors, and told she need not look for a cure till after the change of life. This woman, too, had one paroxysm after giving up drug palliation and making a few changes in her daily habits.

Here were two patients with a "dreadful affliction," which was kept "dreadful" by a senseless and criminal medication—and that, too, by physicians holding degrees from class A colleges.

I refer to these two cases to illustrate what "Anonymous" means by saying: "Few diseases may be cured or ameliorated." Megrim is not cured; and if doping, as these two cases were doped, is ameliorating, some other name should be used in designating the procedure.

CRISES

According to the Toxin Philosophy, every so-called disease is a crisis of Toxemia; which means that toxin has accumulated in the blood above the toleration-point, and the crisis, the so-called disease—call it cold, "flu," pneumonia, headache, or typhoid fever—is a vicarious elimination. Nature is endeavoring to rid the body of toxin. Any treatment that obstructs this effort at elimination baffles nature in her effort at self-curing.

Drugs, feeding, fear, and keeping at work prevent elimination. A cold is driven into chronic catarrh; "flu" may be forced to take on an infected state; pneumonia may end fatally if secretions are checked by drugs; we already know what becomes of headache; typhoid will be forced into a septic state and greatly prolonged, if the patient is not killed.

The above illustrates how "a few cases may be cured or ameliorated." But the story is different when the attending physician *knows* that every so-called disease is a complex of symptoms signifying a crisis of Toxemia—nature's house-cleaning.

[49]

And she—nature—can succeed admirably if not interfered with by venders of poison, who are endeavoring to destroy an imaginary entity lurking somewhere in the system, which are mightily increased and intensified by the venders' cures or amelioratives.

It is a real pleasure for the doctor who knows that he cannot cure anything to watch nature throw off all these symptoms by elimination, if he is willing to do a little "watchful waiting" and "keep hands off." The patient will be comfortable most of the time, and will say, when asked how he is: "I feel all right; I am comfortable." Patients never answer in that way when drugged and fed. Yes, when nature is not hindered by officious professional meddling, sick people can truthfully say, when well over a crisis of house-cleaning: "I had a very comfortable sickness." Nature is not revengeful. Great suffering, chronic and fatal maladies, are built by the incorrigibleness of patients, and the well-meaning but belligerent efforts of the doctors who fight the imaginary foe without ceasing. The people are so saturated with the idea that disease must be fought to a finish that they are not satisfied with conservative treatment. Something must be done, even if they pay for it with their lives, as tens of thousands do every year. This willingness to die on the altar of medical superstition is one very great reason why no real improvement is made in fundamental medical science. When the people demand education—not medication, vaccination, and immunization—they will get it.

Is there nothing for a doctor to do? Yes, of course! He should enter the sick-room with a smile and a cheerful word, free from odors, and neat and clean; be natural, and free from affectations. He should not tell at how many confinements he officiated the night before, or how many thousands he has had in the past ten years. Professional lobbying is not appropriate in the sick-room. Patients should have confidence in their doctor; and if he does a lot of medico-political lying, the patient will know it, and it sloughs confidence.

He should advise an enema daily—a stomach-wash if it is needed; something warm to the feet; perfect quiet; no food, liquid or solid, and positively no drugs, but all the water desired; a warm bath at night; a hot bath when necessary for pain, and as often as necessary to secure comfort. Rest, warmth, fresh air, and quiet are curative. Then the physician should educate his patient into proper living habits, so as to avoid future crises of Toxemia.

When this régime is carried out, and Doctor Nature is allowed full control, the pessimistic statement of "Anonymous" that "a few diseases may be cured or ameliorated" can be changed to read: All acute so-called diseases *can be cured;* and the patient will stay cured if he will practice self-control concerning the enervating habits that brought on his crises of Toxemia. Where this is carried out faithfully, so-called chronic diseases will never be built.

ALL DISEASES ONCE INNOCENT

Cancer, tuberculosis, Bright's disease, and all chronic diseases were once innocent colds "ameliorated," and which returned and were "ameliorated" again and again; each time accompanied by a greater constitutional enervation, and a greater constitutional toleration for toxin-poisoning, requiring a greater requisition of mucous membrane through which to eliminate the toxin.

Research is being carried on vigorously in an attempt to find the cause of disease; the conception of disease being that it is individual. Here is where investigators meet their Waterloo. All the so-called diseases are increasing symptom complexes due to repeated crises of Toxemia. They have no independent existence. As soon as Toxemia is controlled, they disappear, unless an organ has been forced by innumerable crises to degenerate. Even organic change, when the organ is not destroyed, will come back by correcting the life and getting rid of the cause—crises of Toxemia.

To find the cause of cancer, start with colds and catarrh, and watch the pathology as it travels from irritation, catarrh, inflammation, induration, ulceration to cancer.

As well try to find the cause of man by ignoring his conception, embryonic life, childhood, manhood, etc.

All symptoms of all so-called diseases have one origin. All diseases are one. Unity in all things is nature's plan. Polytheism is gone, and everything pertaining to it and coming out of it must go.

HERD-BELIEFS

Few realize man's possibilities if his handicaps are removed—handicaps which are old beliefs and herd-instincts.

The Toxemic Philosophy is founded on the truth that there is no such thing as cure. In this it differs from all the so-called curing systems. Every pretense or promise of cure, in all lines of therapeutics, is false. This cannot be grasped by all minds until time for thinking has allowed the idea to soak in. Convention and superstition have the floor, and they are unwilling to sit down and listen to the other side. Many learn slowly, others not at all, and still others are put to sleep mentally by truth.

There are ox-cart minds in every generation. The recent episode at Dayton, Tennessee, should cure the enthusiasm of those who think the world has outgrown superstition. I have bucked up against medical superstitions of all kinds all my life, and I know that clear-thinking minds are as scarce as hens' teeth. Many compliment me on my clear reasoning on medical subjects; but the moment I cross the border-line into their ethical, moral, and theological preserves, they remind me of my trespassing in no uncertain terms. Even my own profession is quick to ink the waters of my reasoning by declaring that I am an infidel— a word that fills the elect with abhorrence. Who is an infidel? One who rejects a senseless convention. Didn't Christ repudiate the Jehovic cult?

The average mind prefers the old interpretation of words to the "new-fangled" definitions. Until the world agrees on one dictionary, one Bible, and one God, the tempest in the teapot of misunderstanding will continue to ebullate, sending the atomized fundamentalists heavenward and the unatomized modernists hellward.

Of course, God made man. He made everything. But why not find out just how He made him? Surely there is as much "glory to God" in discovering just how He did it as in accepting an infantile interpretation which up to date has got us nowhere. When we know how man is made, we shall understand the laws of his being; and it will not be necessary for him to die of apoplexy, stone in the gall-bladder or kidney, hardening of the arteries, or any other so-called disease caused by breaking the laws of his body and mind.

If we do our duty to our children, shall we teach them the laws of their being and how to respect them, or shall we go on in the same old way, and, when they get sick from breaking the laws of their being and ruin their health, call a surgeon who will cut out God's mistakes? Think it over;

or, if you're too fanatical or bigoted to think, pay
a surgeon to cut out the effects of wrong living,
and continue the cause.

LET US REASON TOGETHER!

Let us do a little homely reasoning. We are
inclined to be awed by the word "infinite." The
infinite is limitless to our limited comprehension—
it is a relative term and ambiguous; but, as we
grow in experience, our once limited comprehen-
sions take on extended dimensions. Each person's
infinite is personal and varies from every other
person's comprehension. We cannot think in
terms of the limitless, and we should not try; for,
if we know the analysis of an atom of salt, we
know the analysis of the infinite amount there is
in the world. This is true of all elements. If we
know the analysis of a pound of butter, we know
the analysis of the infinite amount contained in the
world. If we know all about a man, we know all
about all men. If we know what infinite love is, we
know that infinite love is of the same character.

We should keep our feet on the ground—stay on
earth—and be satisfied that all worlds are like our
world.

HOW TO MEASURE THE INFINITE

We know all by an intensive study of a part.
If we know all about one disease, we know all about
all diseases.

We shall tell the reader all about Toxemia, and

then he should know all about all diseases; for Toxemia is the basic cause of all diseases.

Instead of beginning at the top of any subject, we should begin at the bottom and work up. The usual way for our finite minds is to accept the infinite on faith; then to us the comprehensible does not agree with our preconception, our faith is shocked, our house of belief is divided against itself, and we fall. This is the parting of the ways; and we must reconcile our faith and knowledge by transferring our faith to the belief that the road to all knowledge is by way of the comprehensible. We must either do this or live in doubt concerning the knowable, and accept the unknowable on faith.

Every truth squares itself with every other truth; every department of science and reason blends into a unit. The laws of life are those of the cosmos; the laws of the universe are the laws of God. The road to an understanding of God is from rock to man, and through man to God. Every step must be a block of truth, or God, the goal, will be sidestepped. Behold the head-on collision of the Christian world and the wholesale massacre that took place during the World War—all due to undigested truth. The world is full of truth; but mental indigestion, due to wrong food combinations, is universal.

Many think they know what I mean when I use the word "Toxemia," having referred to the dictionary for its definition.

TOXEMIA, THE BASAL CAUSE OF ALL SO-CALLED
DISEASES

Toxin Poisoning.—Toxin: Any of a class of
poisonous compounds of animal, bacterial, and vegetable origin—any poisonous ptomaine. (Standard Dictionary.)

There are so many ways for the blood to become poisoned that, unless what I mean by "Toxemia" is thoroughly comprehended, there must be
a confused understanding. This explanation is
made necessary because even professional men
have said to me: "Oh, yes, I believe in the poisoning resulting from retained excretions (constipation) and ptomaine (food) poisoning."

As stated before, a ptomaine poisoning resulting from the ingestion of food that has taken on
a state of putrescence, or a poisoning resulting
from this change taking place in food after it has
been eaten, and which is generally called auto-
toxemia, is not an autogenerated poisoning. Both
of these poisons are generated on the outside of
the body, and must be absorbed before the blood
can be poisoned. Food or poison in the intestines
is still on the outside of the body. A suppurating
wound, ulcer, or chancre is on the outside of the
body, and if it causes septic (blood) poisoning, it
will be because the waste-products are not allowed
to drain—to escape. The discharge being ob-
structed, it becomes septic, and its forced absorption poisons the blood. Even vaccinia fails to pro-

[57]

duce septic poisoning, because its poison is discharged on the surface—on the outside of the body. Occasionally the waste-products are forced to enter the blood because of faulty dressings; then septic poisoning, with death, follows.

THE DEADLY GERM

It should not be forgotten that unobstructed free drainage from wounds, ulcers, canals, ducts, keep them aseptic (non-poisonous). The *deadly germ* on the hands, lips, drinking-cups, hanging-straps of street cars—in fact, found anywhere and everywhere—is not deadly until it gets mixed up with man's deadly dirty, filthy physical and mental habits. There are people who cannot be taught cleanliness; they either scrub their bodies raw or neglect them overtime. It is an art to wear clothes and maintain a state of cleanliness conducive to health. Venereal and all skin diseases, including the eruptive fevers, are fostered by clothes. There is something more than prejudice, fanaticism, and partisanship in the continued allusion to the congeneric relationship of syphilis, vaccination, and smallpox. The kinship would have been settled long ago if vaccine and vaccinia were not commericalized. Will those with millions invested, and turning out large dividends, willingly be convinced that they are engaged in the wholesale syphilization of the people? It is not in keeping with our commercialized religion.

The *deadly germ* must be mixed with retained, pent-up waste-products before it becomes metamorphosed into its deadly toxic state. The dog or other animal licks it out of his wound. When the "deadly germ" is osculated into the mouth, and from there into the stomach, it is digested. The normal secretions of the body, on the outside as well as on the inside of the body, are more than enough to get away with all the "deadly germs" allotted to each person.

Normal persons are deadly to all germs and parasites peculiar to the human habitat.

Normal people have no need of heaven or hell; these are conjurations of ignorance and filth on the search for artificial immunization. Truth immunizes the germ fallacy.

Cures and immunization are the products of a civilization that does not civilize. Creedal religion is a cure and an immunization for those who would be good if evil did not betide them.

Self-control and a knowledge of the limitations of our privileges bring to us the best in life; then, if we are contented to live one world at a time, we shall have the best preparation for the tomorrows (future) as they come. If we live well today— live for health of mind and body today—we need not worry about the germs that come tomorrow.

Those who preach fear of germs today are the mental offspring of those who have preached fear of God, devil, hell, and heaven in the past. They do not know that the fear which they inculcate is more to be dreaded than the object of their warning. Fear does a thousand times more harm than any other cause of Toxemia.

Nature goes her limit in the prevention of absorption of any and all poisons. The indurated wall built at the base of ulceration is a conservative measure—it is to prevent absorption. In the matter of prevention, nature sometimes goes too far, and builds tumors and indurations so dense as to obstruct the circulation; then degeneration takes place, with slow absorption of the septic matter. This poisoning takes place very insidiously. It is called cachexia, and the name given to this pathology is syphilis or cancer; or, if of the lungs, it is called tuberculosis.

This may be thought a very great digression from the subject of Toxemia; but, as all pathological roads lead to Rome—the unity of all diseases —an apology is not necessary.

THE MEDICAL WORLD IS LOOKING FOR CURES

The medical world has been looking for a remedy to cure disease, notwithstanding the obvious fact that nature needs no remedy—she needs only an opportunity to exercise her own prerogative of self-healing.

A few years ago a sick doctor offered a million dollars for a cure for cancer. If he had known the cause of disease, instead of being scientifically educated, he would not have died believing in the possibility of a cure, after nature had passed her eternal fiat of unfitness in his case. Cancer is the culmination of years of abuse of nutrition, and years of Toxemia from faulty elimination by forcing the bowels to move. This old and conventional method of so-called elimination may get rid of the accumulation in the bowels, causing an extra amount of water to be thrown out by the kidneys and bowels; but the forcing measure adds to enervation by its overstimulation, and further inhibits elimination proper—elimination of waste-products in the blood, the source of all disease-producing toxins. The most powerful eliminant is a fast. In other words, give nature rest, and she needs no so-called cures. Rest means: Stay in bed, poise mind and body, and fast. Nature then works without handicaps, unless fear is created by all the old fear-mongers, professional and lay, sending to the patient the warning: "It is dangerous to fast; you may never live through it." These wiseacres do not know that there is a vast difference between fasting and starving.

Here is a hint for those kill-joys who are afraid to allow their patients to fast: You know, or think you do, that people who are forced to stay in bed from injury never do well, and this is especially true of old people. Why? Because they are overfed.

GERMS AS A CAUSE OF DISEASE

Germs as a cause of disease is a dying fallacy. The bacteriological deadmarch is on, and those with their ears to the ground can hear it. Intuition is forcing the active medical minds to fortify against the coming revulsion; they are buckling on the armor of endocrinology. Endocrinology, focal infection, autogenous and synthetic remedies, vaccine and serum immunization, are some of the high points in the science of medicine today; but there is a lack of fundamental unity to the system; and nature abhors chaos as she does a vacuum.

Toxemia accepts the germ (organized ferment) as it does the enzyme (unorganized ferment). Both are necessary to health.

My theories have received but little attention except from plagiarists. A few, a very few, physicians know what I stand for. Those few, however, are enthusiastic, and have proved to their own satisfaction that the theory has a universal application. Many attempt to work Toxemia along with some little two-by-four pet curing system—it means petting a little personal pride; but it will not work. Toxemia is big enough for the best in any man.

What more can be asked by any doctor than a philosophy of cause that gives a perfect understanding of the cause of all so-called diseases? To know cause supplies even the layman with a dependable cure and an immunization that immunizes rationally. Dependable knowledge is man's salvation; and when it can be had with as little effort as that required for a thorough understanding of the Philosophy of Toxemia there is little excuse for any man, lay or professional, to hazard ignorance of it.

Toxin—the designating poison in Toxemia—is a product of metabolism. It is a constant, being constantly evolved; and 'when the nerve-energy is normal, it is as constantly eliminated as fast as evolved.

The body is strong or weak, as the case may be, depending entirely on whether the nerve-energy is strong or weak. And it should be remembered that the functions of the body are carried on well or badly according to the amount of energy generated.

IMPORTANCE OF NERVE-ENERGY

Without nerve-energy the functions of the various organs of the body cannot be carried on. Secretions are necessary for preparing the building-up material to take the place of worn-out tissue. The worn-out tissue must be removed—eliminated—from the blood as fast as it is formed, or it accumulates, and, as it is toxic, the system will be poisoned. This becomes a source of enervation.

Elimination of the waste-products of tissue-building is just as necessary as the building-up process. As these two important functions depend on each other, and as both depend on the proper amount of nerve-energy to do their work well, it behooves all people who would enjoy life and health to the full to understand in what way they may be frugal in using nerve-energy so that they may learn how to live conservatively or prudently, thereby enjoying the greatest mental and physical efficiency, and also the longest life. (See chapter on "Enervating Habits.")

To the ignorant, thoughtless, and sensual such suggestions and advice will seem unnecessary, or perhaps the whims or preachments of a crotchety person, or the qualms of a sated sensualist; but it is the writer's belief that the more sober and thoughtful will welcome a knowledge that will help them to become masters of themselves. So far the masses have trusted their health and life to a profession that has failed to make good. I say this advisedly; for now the supposed masters in the profession are looking for the causes of disease, and it should be obvious to any thinking mind that, until the cause of disease is found, certainly no dependable advice can be given as to how to avoid disease.

Fifty-four years of independent thinking, unbiased by sect or creed, have enabled me to discover the true cause of disease; and it is so simple that even a child can learn to protect itself against the said-to-be "diseases peculiar to children."

"These are the times that try men's souls." If Tom Paine were here now, he would change the wording of that line to read: "These are the times that try men's nerves." Nerve-energy and good money are the commodities that are spent very rapidly these days. Chasing the dollar causes great waste of energy; and the dollar has been chased so much that it has developed wanderlust to such a degree that men enervate themselves catching up with a few, but prostrate themselves endeavoring to break them of their wander-habit. There are many ways to use up nerve-energy. It should be the ambition of everybody to conserve all the nerve-energy possible for the extraordinary amount required to keep the speeding-up necessary to adjust humanity to the automobile pace. This will come in time.

Man adjusted himself to the change from the ox-cart; Dobbin the flea-bitten, string-halt, and blind, and the steamboats, on which our forebears took their honeymoon trips, to the "steam-cars" and high-stepping bays and family carriage.

Many will go into the hands of the receiver before the nervous system becomes adjusted to high-power automobiles and flying-machines.

Without nerve-energy the functions of the body cannot be carried on properly. The present-day strenuousness causes enervation, which checks elimination, and the retained toxins bring on Toxemia.

Everything that acts on the body uses up energy. Cold and heat require the expenditure of nerve-energy to adjust the body to the changes.

After middle life, those who would keep well and live to be old must have a care concerning keeping warm and avoiding chilling of the body. They must let up on table pleasures and practice self-restraint in all ways. Allowing the feet to be cold for any length of time—allowing the body to chill when a top-coat would prevent—is using up nerve-energy very fast.

Work with worry will soon end in flagging energy—enervation.

As no provision is made for the demand of an extra supply of energy at a given time, it is necessary, very necessary, to know how to conserve what we have and build more.

CONSERVATION OF ENERGY THE GREATEST THERAPEUTIC MEASURE

Now that I have found that enervation is the source of the cause of the only disease (Toxemia) to which mankind is heir, it is easy to see that the so-called science of medicine, as practiced, is an ally extraordinary of all the causes of enervation, and becomes a builder of disease instead of curing or ameliorating man's sufferings. Every so-called cure in its very nature causes enervation. Even the drugs used to relieve pain end in making a greater pain, and sometimes kill. The drugs to relieve cough in pneumonia sometimes kill the patient. Removing stone from the gall-bladder does not cure the cause, and more stones form.

Rest from habits that enervate is the only way to put nature in line for curing. Sleep and rest of body and mind are necessary to keep a sufficient supply of energy. Few people in active life rest enough.

Enervation per se is not disease. Weakness, lost power, is not disease; but, by causing a flagging of the elimination of tissue-waste, which is toxic, the blood becomes charged with toxin, and this we call Toxemia—poison in the blood. This is disease, and when the toxin accumulates beyond the toleration-point, a crisis takes place; which means that the poison is being eliminated. This we call disease, but it is not. The only disease is Toxemia, and what we call diseases are the symptoms produced by a forced vicarious elimination of toxin through the mucous membrane.

When the elimination takes place through the mucous membrane of the nose, it is called a cold—Catarrh of the nose; and where these crises are repeated for years, the mucous membrane thickens and ulcerates, and the bones enlarge, closing the passage, etc. At this stage hay-fever or hay-asthma develops. When the throat and tonsils, or any of the respiratory passages, become the seat of the crises of Toxemia, we have croup, tonsilitis, pharyngitis, laryngitis, bronchitis, asthma, pneumonia, etc. What is in a name? All are symptoms of the expulsion of toxin from the blood at the different points named, and are essentially of the same character and evolving from the one cause —namely, Toxemia—crises of Toxemia.

This description can be extended to every organ

of the body; for any organ that is enervated below the average standard from stress of habit, from work or worry, from injury, or from whatever cause, may become the location of crises of Toxemia. The symptoms presented differ with each organ affected; and that gives color to the belief that every symptom-complex is a separate and distinct disease. But, thanks to the new light shed upon nomenclature (naming disease) by the Philosophy of Toxemia, every symptom-complex goes back to the one and only cause of all so-called diseases—namely, Toxemia.

The symptoms that are called gastritis (catarrh of the stomach) are very unlike the symptoms of cystitis (catarrh of the urinary bladder); yet both are caused by crises of Toxemia—both become the locations for the vicarious elimination of toxin from the blood.

It should be obvious to the discerning how extraordinarily illogical it is to treat a catarrh of the nose as a local disease; or, when crises are repeated until ulceration takes place, and the mucous membrane becomes so sensitive that dust and pollen cause sneezing and watering of the eyes—symptoms called hay-fever—to treat these symptoms as a distinct disease caused by pollen. Rest and total abstinence from food, liquid and solid, and reforming all enervating habits, will restore nerve-energy; the elimination of toxin through the natural channels will take place, and full health will return. This state will remain permanently if the erstwhile victim of hay-fever, or any other so-called disease, will "stay put."

The first elimination of toxin through the nose is called a cold. When this elimination is continuous, with exacerbation—toxin crises (fresh colds)—occasionally, ulceration takes place, bony spurs form, and hay-fever develops. These are all symptoms of toxin elimination. The cause is the same from the first cold to hay-fever. The catarrhal discharge that continues throughout the interims of fresh colds (crises of Toxemia) is chronic catarrh, named such in medical nomenclatures, and treated locally as though it were an independent, fiendish entity; when the truth is that the victim of so-called *chronic catarrh* keeps his system enervated by tobacco, alcohol, sugar and sweets of all kinds, coffee, tea, excessive eating of butter and bread, too much rich cooking, excessive eating of all foods, excess of sensual pleasures, etc. (See chapter on "Causes of Enervation.")

Keeping the system enervated prevents the reestablishment in full of elimination through the normal excretory organs. The organism, as time runs on, becomes more tolerant of toxin, and the "catching-cold habit" shows fewer (colds) crises of Toxemia. A greater number of the mucous membranes are requisitioned to carry out vicarious elimination. The whole organism begins to show deterioration. The so-called chronic diseases begin to manifest. In catarrh of the stomach the mucous membrane takes on thickening, hardening, ulceration, and cancer—all described in the nomenclature of medical science as so many distinctive diseases. But they are no more distinctive than President Washington was distinct from the boy George who cut down his father's cherry tree. Cancer was once the symptom-complex of a so-called cold; but, according to the Philosophy of Toxemia, it is the end of many crises of Toxemia. As the crises continued, symptoms changed, in accordance with the organic degeneration caused by the crises of Toxemia.

Every so-called disease has the same inception, evolution, and maturity, differing only as the organic structure involved differs.

Treating the various symptom-complexes as distinct entities is fully as scientific as salving the end of a dog's tail for its sore ear.

All diseases are the same fundamentally.

The cause travels back to Toxemia, caused by enervation, which checked elimination; and enervating habits of body and mind are the primary causes of lost resistance—enervation.

Every chronic disease starts with Toxemia and a toxemic crisis. The crises are repeated until organic changes take place. The chain of symptoms range from cold or catarrh to Bright's disease, tuberculosis, cancer, syphilis, ataxia, and other so-called diseases; all, from beginning to end, symptoms of the cumulative effects of crises of Toxemia.

Enervation Is General

EVERYBODY was surprised at the large percentage of our young manhood plucked by the medical examining boards during the World War. To that surprise, add the one which the Philosophy of Toxemia adds, and thinking people should be applauded.

The examining boards passed all young men who did not show a developed pathology; which meant all who did not show some change of organ or tissue—structural change.

When it is known that functional derangements precede structural changes by months and even years, it should be quite obvious that there were more young men passed by the boards who were potentially ill or unable to carry on than were plucked. Time has proven this generally unknown fact true; for before the war was over ninety-five per cent of the American army had received hospital attention for sickness, other than injury, from once to five times. And the boys who did not get over to France died by the thousands from the "flu."

What does this mean? It means that life as it is lived causes the people generally to be enervated. And when nerve-energy drops below normal, the elimination of toxin—a natural product of metabolism—is checked, and is retained in the blood, bringing on Toxemia—the first, last, *and only efficient* cause of all so-called diseases.

It should be obvious to discerning minds that the amount of toxin in the blood must vary with each individual, and that the degree of resistance also must vary with each individual. An amount that would cause a toxemic crises in one would apparently have no effect on another. An enervating cause—the usual immunization—that would scarcely produce a reaction at one time in a given subject might send the same subject to a hospital at another time, or even be fatal instanter. *Active anaphylaxis is the alibi or apology of the pro-vaccinators;* but it does not change the fact that vaccines are poisons, even if they are "pure," regardless of the iterated and reiterated protests that they are innocent and harmless.

The amount of harm done the army by vaccination and re-revaccination will never be known. No words can describe the harm that immunizing with vaccines and serums has done and is doing, except wholesale vandalism.

The average doctor cannot think, and the others do not dare to think except conventionally out loud. I do not know where to place the men of the medical profession who are capable of thinking, but who refuse to allow reason to guide them in their thinking in the matter of so-called immunization. Can class-consciousness or class-bigotry explain? Surely knavishness is unfit. It has been said of me, because of my stand against the germ theory and vaccination, that I have "peculiar views;" by some, that I am "an ignoramus." If I am, it is strange that fundamentally I find my thoughts and beliefs running parallel with one of the greatest thinkers of the nineteenth century—the famous English philosopher Herbert Spencer. I was browsing in my library a few days ago, and picked up "Facts and Comments." I turned to "Vaccination," and in it found more worth-while, constructive thought, in a short essay of less than three pages, than can be found in all medical literature on the same subject. I have decided to quote the whole essay, and I shall be pleased if others get the mental kick out of it that I have enjoyed:

"When once you interfere with the order of nature, there is no knowing where the results will end," was the remark made in my presence by a distinguished biologist. There immediately escaped from him an expression of vexation at his lack of reticence; for he saw the various uses I might make of the admission.

Jenner and his disciplines have assumed that when the vaccine virus has passed through a patient's system he is safe, or comparatively safe, against smallpox, and that there the matter ends. I will not here say anything for or against this assumption.* I merely propose to

---

*Except, indeed, by quoting the statement of a well-known man, Mr. Kegan Paul, the publisher, respecting his own experience. In his "Memoirs" (pp. 260-61) he says, respecting his smallpox when adult: "I had had smallpox when a child, in spite of vaccination, and had been vaccinated but a short time before. I am the third of my own immediate family who have had smallpox twice, and with whom vaccination has always taken."

show that there the matter does *not* end. The interference with the order of nature has various sequences other than that counted upon. Some have been made known.

A Parliamentary Return issued in 1880 (No. 392) shows that, comparing the quinquennial periods 1847-1851 and 1874-1878, there was in the latter a diminution in the deaths from all causes of infants under one year old of 6,600 per million births per annum; while the mortality caused by eight specified diseases, either directly communicable or exacerbated by the effects of vaccination, increased from 20,524 to 41,353 per million births per annum—more than double. It is clear that far more were killed by these other diseases than were saved from smallpox.†

To the communication of diseases thus demonstrated must be added accompanying effects. It is held that the immunity produced by vaccination implies some change in the components of the body—a necessary assumption. But now, if the substances composing the body, solid or liquid or both, have been so modified as to leave them no longer liable to smallpox, is the modification otherwise inoperative? Will anyone dare to say that it produces no further effect than that of shielding the patient from a particular disease? You cannot change the constitution in relation to one invading agent and leave it unchanged in regard to all other invading agents. What must the change be? There are cases of unhealthy persons in whom a serious disease, as typhoid fever, is followed by improved health. But these are not normal

---

†This was in the days of arm-to-arm vaccination, when medical men were certain that other diseases (syphilis, for instance) could not be communicated through the vaccine virus. Anyone who looks into the Transactions of the Epidemiological Society of some thirty years ago will find that they were suddenly convinced to the contrary by a dreadful case of wholesale syphilization. In these days of calf-lymph vaccination, such dangers are excluded; not that of bovine tuberculosis, however. But I name the fact as showing what amount of faith is to be placed in medical opinion.

cases; if they were, a healthy person would become more healthy by having a succession of diseases.* Hence, as a constitution modified by vaccination is not made more able to resist perturbing influences in general, it must be made less able. Heat and cold and wet and atmospheric changes tend ever to disturb the balance, as do also various foods, excessive exertion, mental strain. We have no means of measuring alterations in resisting power, and hence they commonly pass unremarked. There are, however, evidences of a general relative debility. Measles is a severer disease than it used to be, and deaths from it are very numerous. Influenza yields proof. Sixty years ago, when at long intervals an epidemic occurred, it seized but few, was not severe, and left no serious sequelæ; now it is permanently established, affects multitudes in extreme forms, and often leaves damaged constitutions. The disease is the same, but there is less ability to withstand it.

There are other significant facts. It is a familiar biological truth that the organs of sense and the teeth arise out of the dermal layer of the embryo. Hence abnormalities affect all of them; blue-eyed cats are deaf, and hairless dogs have imperfect teeth. ("Origin of Species," Chap. 1.) The like holds of constitutional abnormalities caused by disease. Syphilis in its earlier stages is a skin disease. When it is inherited, the effects are malformation of teeth, and in later years iritis (inflammation of the iris). Kindred relations hold with other skin diseases; instance the fact that scarlet fever is often accompanied by loosening of the teeth, and the fact that with measles often go disorders—sometimes temporary, sometimes permanent—of both eyes and ears. May it not be thus with another skin disease—that which vaccination gives? If so, we have an explanation of the

---

*Toxemia explains this phenomenon.—Ed.

frightful degeneracy of teeth among young people in recent times; and we need not wonder at the prevalence of weak and defective eyes among them. Be these suggestions true or not, one thing is certain: The assumption that vaccination changes the constitution in relation to smallpox, and does not otherwise change it, is sheer folly.

"When once you interfere with the order of nature, there is no knowing where the results will end."

Interfering with the order of nature is a vast subject—one without end; but nature comes smiling through, except when overwhelmed. Health—good health—is a greater force than bad—than every interference—and can correct every evil effect that is not fatal, if the influence is removed.

Stimulants, continued over a long period, cause a gradual deterioration, and finally, unless the habit is stopped, end fatally. Toxin is a stimulant and a natural product of metabolism. When the body is normal, the toxin is removed as fast as generated; but when any enervating habit is practiced beyond the power of recuperation, the toxin accumulates, and Toxemia is established—which means that the body has lost its protecting power. Now, if vaccine or any infection gains entrance into the blood, "there is no knowing where the effects will end."

Toxemia throws light on this perplexing point. When an infection takes place in a person with normal resistance, creating a vaccinia—a local

[76]

skin inflammation—and pus-formation occurs, it usually ends with the healing of the abcess. If inoculation of smallpox virus is made in the Jennerian way, by inserting the virus subcutaneously —splitting the skin and rubbing it in—violent septic infection takes place, causing death in many cases. Laws were passed in England many years ago prohibiting this practice.

In toxemic subjects, a local infection set up by the virus of sepsis from any source—vaccination, a badly cared-for injury, a wound that fails to drain, an infected tooth, sinus, etc.—causes a septic fever of a malignant type, which is liable to end in death or in invalidism. A system badly enervated and toxemic, has little power to resist; and when the blood is very toxemic, it is very vulnerable to the influence of any infection.

Where the infection is not so malignant as to overwhelm the system, due to the virulence of the infecting agent, or to the enervation and toxemic state being so great as to have destroyed resistance, the patient may rally from the crisis and get well under the proper management. If, however, the management is bad, the patient may linger in a state of semi-invalidism for a few months or years, and finally die.

Mr. Roosevelt's illness and taking-off at least twenty-five years too soon was a pronounced type of such derangement. The great and forceful man was pronouncedly toxemic. He was injured, as everybody knows, on one of his trips into the jungles. Infection took place, which probably would have killed a less robust man. He returned home, and continued his enervating habits, preventing his fine body from cleaning house.

Such cases can be brought back to the normal, but never under conventional treatment.

When toxemic subjects are infected, the infection will never be eliminated entirely until enervation and Toxemia are overcome. Unless patients of this character are put to bed and fasted until elimination is completed, then fed properly, and taught how to eat within their limitations, and unless they are willing to give up all enervating habits, there is no hope of their ever getting well. These subjects often develop tuberculosis, Bright's disease, and other lingering so-called diseases. Our federal hospitals are full of young men who will never get well; for Toxemia is developed faster than it is thrown off.

Nature's order is interfered with by enervating habits until Toxemia is established; then a vaccination, or an infection from any source, acts sooner or later as a firebrand in causing the most vulnerable organ to take on organic change. The organ, however, has nothing to do with cause, and directing treatment to the organ is compounding nonsense. Types of such nonsense are blood-transfusion for pernicious anemia; gland treatment for gland impotency; cutting out stones, ulcers, tumors, etc.

There is no question but that one of the most

pernicious practices in vogue today is treating so-called disease with disease, and immunizing with the products of disease.

One of the first things to do to get rid of any so-called disease is to get rid of Toxemia; for it is this state of the blood that makes disease possible. Infection, drug- and food-poisoning may kill; but if they do not, they will be short-lived in a subject free from enervation and Toxemia. Conversely, the poisoning will linger in the system until Toxemia is overcome; then elimination will remove all traces of infection.

Syphilitic infection in a pronouncedly toxemic subject is thrown into great virulency by conventional treatment. The infection is the least offender of the trio. Add fear and wrong eating, and we have a formidable symptom-complex, justifying all that professional syphilomaniacs say and write about the disease. Remove Toxemia, drugging, fear, and vile eating, and there is little left. What there is can easily be thrown out by nature.

WE are builders of tomorrow, and we need not pay a fortune-teller—a doctor, lawyer, preacher, banker—to tell us what will happen to us tomorrow. ¶Nothing will happen. The inevitable will come. We shall inherit the fruits of today's sowing.

Poise

THE state or quality of being balanced. Figuratively, equanimity; repose.

Equanimity—Evenness of mind or temper; composure; calmness. (Standard Dictionary.)

I presume that, to be technically poised, we should be anatomically, physiologically, and chemically balanced; but, as asymmetry is the rule, we cannot hope to be balanced. We can, however, strive for equanimity—evenness of mind and temper.

Contentment comes with striving, not with possession. Apparently this is not always true; for we see people very dissatisfied and unhappy who are busy.

Someone has said: "Blessed is the man who has found his work." This means that he is fully occupied and contented with his work, not its emoluments. No man is satisfied with work that has nothing in it but the dollars he gets out of it. Nothing but creative work satisfies the mind.

What is there in it? Advancement, self-development, and a chance in the future to do good are about as little as will satisfy ambition.

To make for contentment, the work must occupy and satisfy the mind. Idle minds are dissatisfied minds. If asked what prescription I would give children to secure their future happiness, I would say: Teach them to love work! work! work! We have overworked the old saying: "All work and no play makes Jack a dull boy." Now it is reversed to: "All play and no work makes Jack a bandit."

If parents cannot keep children busy, the city, county, or state should furnish work—not in industrial schools, but the work that is best suited to each child. A child must be busy. Christ got busy at twelve years of age and earlier. We must be busy.

As I said, contentment comes with striving, not with possession. This is a law of psychology as well as of physics. We should be happy that we are not contented; for, if we were, we should not have anything to overcome—no reason for striving —and, of course, fail to enjoy the work and labor of attaining.

Man never is, but always to be blest. (Pope.)

Because Pope made that statement, it should not be taken too seriously. I have found many people blest who did not know it. There are more blessings in disguise than are found in the lime-light. One of the commonest blessings of mankind is that about ninety-nine per cent of our wants we never realize. If most people could cut out time as often as they wish, their lives would be greatly shortened: "I wish it were this time next year." "I wish now were ten years from now; I should then be through college and established in business."

The disposition of most people is to seek abridgement. Nature abhors a vacuum, and that is what abridgements are. "Get-Rich-Quick Wallingford" is the ideal of all.

Short-cuts to success; salesmanship that means coercing the vacillating—those of weak will, those who can be persuaded to buy prematurely, those who do not know their own minds; in short, inducing people to buy what they do not need and cannot afford is called good salesmanship. What is the matter with the people today? General indebtedness. The sales-people have made more than they know how to spend wisely on themselves—they do not know how to fill their vacuums. Those who have been persuaded to run in high when they should have stayed in low—or, what would have been better, continued to ride a bicycle or remained on foot—are distressed because of premature supply. Both extremes lack poise, and build restlessness and dissatisfaction. The automobile is a necessity; but it has been forced into a luxury that has far outrun necessity. It has built great fortunes at one end, and marked poverty at the other end, that will create a financial disease called panic, unless remedied soon. Panic is another name for a vacuum which will be filled with much unhappiness.

Getting through school without filling in the time well, by short-cuts, ponies, and favoritism, builds vacuity. Time and honest labor are necessary for building character, education, and ability in any and all lines. In the physical as well as in the mental world the old Latin apothegm applies: *Cito maturum, cito putridum*—"Soon ripe, soon rotten." Athletes die early. Why? Development is forced. Excessive use of the muscular system forces an extra supply of blood to the muscles. This in turn forces an extra supply of food to meet the demand of waste and supply. Overstimulation enervates, and the toxin fails to be carried out as rapidly as formed; hence Toxemia is established, which gradually brings on degeneration of heart and blood-vessels. "No chain is stronger than its weakest link." In athletics, the strongest links are in constant use for all the strength they have. The stability that youth gives tissue is rapidly ageing, with the result that the athlete dies of senility in youth. Fitzsimmons was called the "grand old man of the ring" at thirty-five. In this saying, which was meant to be a compliment to the king of athletes, was an expression of scientific knowledge beyond understanding in the sporting world—subconsciously building better than they knew; for in reality he had aged himself by stressing his body.

Youth wants to move faster than good, substantial growth justifies. Young professional men are in hot-haste to succeed their predecessors, always confident that they can do more than fill their places.

Today inexperience is hot-footing civilization to a quick maturity, and obviously to a premature end. Hot-haste has ill-prepared even those with age to be safe advisers. Knowledge not seasoned by time, experience, and poise never matures.

Poise and equanimity have become meaningless terms in this age. The elements of success which make for ideal maturity are lacking in the welding influence of time and experience. The present-day mind is athletic; it is prematurely aged at the expense of time, which is required for stabilizing. Hospitals, penitentiaries, and insane asylums cannot be built fast enough to accommodate the prematurely senile. That is what disease is—old-age tissue outrunning the supply of new.

Too many abridgments, from the kindergarten to the high school and on through college, leave vacuums to be filled by the lies of civilization, and the disease and unhappiness that false knowledge and immature judgment bring.

Personal peculiarities, affectations, and petty habits of all kinds are boomerangs that return to poison life's sweet dreams.

Nature smiles on those who are natural; but those who persist in grimacing, mentally or physically, she joins in a conspiracy to distort them at their pleasure. We can be happy and contented, or we can be unhappy and discontented. We can make our choice, and nature will do the rest.

I just came from a drug-store into which I had stepped to purchase a tube of camphor ice. The druggist fumbled, and, being self-conscious, his self-pity made it necessary for him to say that he was feeling bad and had been lying down most of the afternoon. He accompanied his remarks with a sick grimace of his features and a bodily expression of weakness. He, no doubt, would have enjoyed discussing his discomforts with me, but I ignored the subject and passed out. He is cultivating a sick habit that will spoil his life and make of him a bore to all except those who frequent his shop hunting cures. "Misery loves company." People with the sick habit flock together, and never appear to tire recounting and comparing their discomforts. The most insignificant symptoms are retained in memory for years. Self-pity causes them to exaggerate, and in time they believe the worst possible about themselves. Such a life is ruined, unless complete reformation is made. This state of mind brings on enervation and Toxemia. The symptoms are a general nervousness, indigestion, constipation, coated tongue, anxiety concerning cancer or some other malady that may prove fatal. The muscular system is more or less tensed. The constipation is accompanied by an abnormal contraction of the rectum. The entire body is abnormally tense. Such patients have difficulty in going to sleep, and when they are about to drop off to sleep they are awakened with a jerk—a violent contraction of all the muscles. These people are light sleepers, and complain that they do not sleep at all. A few complain of headache and nausea. They are imitators, and often develop new symptoms after reading about disease or listening to others relating their symptoms.

Many of these cases of neurosis are operated upon for various supposed abdominal derangements. Too often doctors treat such people for what they say is the matter with them. Occasionally we find self-sacrificing, amiable women who are never robust, but who live and work beyond their strength for others. These mothers in early life had ambitions for a career, and the dissappointment brought on a profound enervation, permanently impairing nutrition; for the one great sorrow prevented a full return to normal. Fortunately, surcease was found in doing for others; and in time making others happy became a vicarious nepenthe so perfect that those whom they soothed with their sweet smiles and cheering words often said: "Aunt Mary, you must have lived a charmed life in which no sorrow ever entered." The answer would be more smiles and encouragement.

Those who find a life of service to take the place of ambition's jilts have made no mistake in the selection of the Great Physician; but those who seek cures outside of self are hunting cures in a Fool's Paradise.

Cures! There are no cures. The subsconscious builds health or disease according to our order.

If we send impulses of irritation, discontent, unhappiness, complaining, hate, envy, selfishness, greed, lust, etc., the subconscious builds us in the image of our order.

If we send to the sub-conscious sensual impulses, our order is returned to us blear-eyed, with swollen features, headaches, bad breath, pain here, pain there, blurred intellect, carelessness in business, of friends, and of self. We interpret our state as disease, and send for a doctor, who finds albumin in the urine, rheumatism in the joints, a leaky heart, threatened apoplexy, dropsy, *et al.* We take his dope, his operations, his immunizations; but we continue to send sensual impulses— big dinners, strong cigars, lascivious indulgences. The doctor does no good. Another and another is sent for. Skillful examinations are given. Syphilis is found. Synthetic drugs are prescribed. Other doctors examine, who find tuberculosis. And at last real skill is detected in a physician who finds *cancer.* But all the time our orders are going to the subconscious, and the returns are made faithfully in the image of our maker.

The truth is that we are not needing a doctor at all. We need a physician who will effect a reconciliation between our subconscious maker and ourselves. What we need is to be taught self-control, poise, equanimity, repose. And when these impulses are sent over the sympathetic nerves to our subconscious maker, we shall begin to receive images of a more ideal man, until an approach to perfection is attained.

Self-control, with an ideal of just the kind of person we should like to be held before the subconscious all the time, will be returned to us just as we order. We are made in the image of the ideal we hold before our maker—the subconscious. We must live it, however. Simply holding an ideal will not get us anywhere. If our ideal is for sobriety, getting drunk will not bring our dreams true. If our ideal is for perfect health, we certainly cannot expect a sensual life to build it.

We may have an image, but if we do not live it, a distortion will be created.

A grunting, complaining habit builds that kind of an individual.

If we refuse to live composed, poised, and relaxed, we become tense and build discomfort. A contracted brow builds headache. A tense, fixed state of the muscular system brings on muscle-fatigue, which may be treated as neuralgia, neuritis, or rheumatism. A slight injury to any part of the body, coddled, nursed, and kept without motion, may start a fixation of the muscles, causing more pain from muscle-fatigue than from the injury.

Enough neurotics have been relieved and cured of muscle-fatigue to put two schools of spine manipulators in good standing with the people.

All through the ages mountebanks, magnetic

healers, and various cults of "laying on of hands" have worked among people who had time to nurse a slight injury into a very large fatigue disease. Fortunes have been made out of vile-smelling liniments because of the supposed cures made by rubbing the dope on sprained backs and joints. The same cures could have been made by simply rubbing the parts; but the minds that go with spineless people, who have time to wait for miraculous cures, could not be made to believe that a cure could be effected without that mysterious healing property associated with evil-looking and vile-smelling medicaments.

A sensitive, insignificant pile tumor may set up such a tense state of the entire muscular system as to render the subject a confirmed invalid. Such a case became a patient of mine a few weeks ago. On examination, I found an extreme contraction of the sphincter muscles. His entire body was tense, and, of course, he had muscle-fatigue, which caused him to believe that he was a very sick man. I had him lie down, and I taught him how to relax; then I introduced a finger into his rectum—very slowly, to avoid giving pain as much as possible. I was about thirty minutes bringing relaxation of the anal muscles. While manipulating, I was advising relaxation of his body. Before he left my office he declared that he felt better than he had for two years, notwithstanding the fact that he had been in a hospital and otherwise treated most of that time. I gave him instructions on how to poise and how to manipulate the rectum and anus.

All his stomach troubles, and discomforts generally, passed away in a week.

I have seen many invalids of nervous type who had been treated by many doctors and for many diseases. Tension of the entire body was one of the pronounced symptoms, and health could not be brought back until this habit was overcome.

The discomforts complained of by those who have tumor of the womb, goiter, cystitis, stomach and bowel derangements, rest largely on a basis of nervous tension, which must be overcome before comfort and full health will return.

Position in standing, walking, sitting, and lying down may be such as to cause tension. We have occupational diseases and emotional diseases; and lack of poise complicates all of these so-called diseases and brings on tension.

Children are prone to become nervous and excited when tired. When allowed to eat heartily, when excited and tired, they have indigestion. Extreme cases develop convulsions. Fear and anxiety are two elements that lead on to chorea.

Poise of mind and body should receive attention early as well as late in life.

Good health late in life indicates self-control, moderation in all things, and equanimity—poise.

Moderation does not mean the same to all people. Some men call three to six cigars a day moderate indulgence; others believe that one to six a month is temperate. Those who have an irritable heart and stomach are immoderate when they use tobacco at all.

Fortunate is the person who knows his limitations and respects them. Of such a person may be said that he is poised.

IMMUNIZATION

Wouldn't it be incongruous if in the evolution of man such an important element as auto-immunization should be left out? No animal has been forgotten in the great scheme of creation. Powers of offense and defense have been wisely provided, and to suppose that the king of all animals—man—should be left defenseless is most absurd. No, man is provided with a nervous system, at the head of which is a brain capable of thinking, which can come to the aid of a flagging nervous system and help to renew it.

When the nervous system is normal—when there is full nerve-energy—man is normal and immune to disease. Disease begins to manifest only when environments and personal habits use up energy faster than it is renewed. This contingency the properly educated mind begins to remedy at once by removing or overcoming all enervating influences.

Man's immunization to disease requires a life so well ordered that his nerve-energy is kept at or near normal. When nerve-energy is prodigally squandered, he is forced into a state of enervation; then elimination of the waste-products is checked, leaving the waste—toxin—in the blood, causing Toxemia or self-poisoning—the first, last, and only true disease that man is heir to. All other poisons are accidental and evanescent, and without Toxemia can have no entree to the system. Poisons may be swallowed, infected, or inoculated into the body, and poison or even kill; but such an experience is not to be classed as disease, any more than a broken leg or a gunshot wound.

Toxin is a normal, natural product of the system, always present. Being a constant, it answers every requirement for a universal cause of all so-called diseases. All the different symptom-complexes, which are given special names, take their names from the organs involved in the toxin crisis; but they are not individual—they are only symptoms of the vicarious elimination. For example: Tonsilitis, gastritis, bronchitis, pneumonia, colonitis, are each and every one Toxemic crises, differing only in location and symptoms. So-called diseases are just so many different locations where toxin is being eliminated. All are different manifestations of one disease—Toxemia.

Toxemia is the only explanation of why so many young men were refused by the examining boards during the late war. Many were sent over to France who soon found the hospital; for they were near the limit of their toxin-resistance. The excitement used up their nerve-energy. The enervation was quickly followed by Toxemia. Their sicknesses were given names; but the truth was that they had Toxemia, and their diseases were crises of Toxemia, which means vicarious elimination.

After the numerous vaccinations to which the boys were subjected on entering the army, probably fear or apprehension was next in order of enervating influences.

DIAGNOSIS A MEDICAL DELUSION

Diagnosing according to *modern medical science* is a scheme of symptomatology that means nothing except a guide in discovering organic change—pathological change; and if no change or pathology is found, the case is sent home, with the advice to return again in a few months; or perhaps it will be kept under observation for a while. Even cases presenting pathological changes, such as we see in rheumatic arthritis, I have known of being sent home for six months, because no point of infection could be found. The patient would be sent away with the statement: "After a thorough examination, we cannot find the cause of your disease. Come back in about six months, and it may be showing up in that time." So much for the influence that focal infection has on the mind of the profession. Suppose infected teeth were found, or sinus infection, what of it? What causes the teeth and sinuses to be infected? Why is rheumatism a symptom of infection, and the focal infections not a symptom of rheumatism?

The truth is that rheumatism, infected teeth,

[93]

and sinus infections, as well as every other pathology found in the body, are effects. Symptoms without lesions represent functional derangements which have not been repeated long enough or often enough to cause organic change. If, as diagnosis goes, the cause is to be found in the disease, at what stage are we to look for it? Is it at the beginning, or in the fully developed organic change, or in the dead man? Mackenzie believed that it should be looked for at the very beginning, which meant with him the earliest change. He believed that an intensive study at this stage would discover cause. This was a mistaken idea of his, which is proved by the fact that the cause of rheumatism and cancer cannot be found early or late, and that those who believe germs cause disease cannot find them until pathology is found. It appears to me, after being in the game for over fifty years, that a plan which has received so much labor without reward should be abandoned.

Diagnosis is so fraught with the element of uncertainty that no reliance can be placed upon it.

Research occupies an army of laboratory experts in hunting the cause of disease, and also cures. They are doomed to fail; for how is it possible to find cause in effects?

The specialist is so limited in his knowledge of the philosophy of health and disease that he becomes deluded on the subject; and this delusion often causes him to see meningitis, appendicitis, ovaritis—or any disease that happens to be the subject of his specialty—in every case brought to him. As a matter of fact, most attacks of disease of any and all kinds get well, whether treated or not.

This statement needs a little explanation. It is said that eighty per cent who fall sick get well, or could get well without the aid of a doctor. All so-called attacks of disease of whatever kind are crises of Toxemia, which means vicarious elimination of Toxin that has accumulated above the satu-ration (toleration) point. These crises may be symptoms which we call cold, "flu," tonsilitis, gas-tritis, headache, or some other light malady. They come today and are gone in a few days. If treated, we say they were cured. If they are not treated, we say they got well without treatment. The truth is that the surplus toxin — the amount accumulated above the point which can be main-tained with comfort—is eliminated, and comfort returns. This is not a cure; it is one of nature's palliations. When the cause or causes of enerva-tion are discovered and removed, the nerve-energy returns to normal. Elimination removes toxin as fast as developed by metabolism. This is health—this is all there is to any cure. In a few words: Stop all enervating habits; stop eating; rest until nerve-energy is restored to normal. When this is accomplished, the patient is cured. A short or long fast is beneficial to most sick people. Those who are afraid of fasting should not fast. All other so-called cures are a delusion, and at the most a passing palliation; but enough such cures are performed daily to keep a large army of doctors and cultists in bread, butter, and a degree of respectability. Their cured patients, however, glacier-like, move steadily down to the river Styx —thousands and thousands of them years before their time, many even before their prime, and all maintaining a false belief concerning what disease is, and a more foolish notion concerning cures.

TOXEMIA SIMPLIFIES THE UNDERSTANDING OF DISEASE

When a child shows symptoms of high fever, pain, and vomiting, what is the disease? It may be indigestion from overeating or eating improper food. It may be the beginning of gastritis, scarlet fever, diphtheria, meningitis, infantile paralysis, or some other so-called disease. The treatment, according to the Philosophy of Toxemia, may be positive and given with confidence. There need be no waiting for developments, no guessing, no mistakes. What is done is the correct treatment for any so-called disease, named or not named. Get rid of the exciting causes, whatever they are. Ninety-nine times out of a hundred the stomach and bowels are full of undigested food. Wash out the bowels, and get rid of this source of infection. Then give a hot bath of sufficient duration to furnish complete relief from any pain. When discomfort returns, give another bath. Use an enema every day, and twice daily if symptoms demand.

So long as there is fever, rest assured that the bowels are not cleaned out. Provide plenty of fresh air and water, and keep the patient quiet. See to it that nothing but water goes into the stomach until the fever and discomfort are entirely overcome; then give very light food at first.

A child that is given meat and eggs and an excess of milk is liable to develop putrefactive diseases. It is doubtful (and I believe impossible) if any child brought up on fruit, whole wheat and other grains, and vegetables can ever evolve diphtheria, scarlet fever, or smallpox, or develop septic fever—typhoid.

The methods of the regular practice of medicine are in keeping with the habits of body and mind that lead to malignant diseases, epidemics, etc. As a man thinketh, so is he.

The regular profession believes in antitoxin, vaccine, and autogenous remedies; and these remedies fit the psychology of a mode of living that leads to vicious types of disease.

Most people are in sympathy with impossible cures—cures without removing causes.

All so-called cures will some day be proved a delusion. Remember that children will not be sick if they are not toxemic. Let the local manifestations be what they may, the basic cause is always the same—Toxemia plus septic infection; and if this state is not added to by food, cases treated in this way will be aborted—jugulated, if you please. Doctors who have seen only regular practice will

declare that the cases recovering in this manner are irregular and lacking in intenstiy. Of course, they are not typical; for they have not been complicated with fear and disease-building treatment.

Doctors will say: "Suppose it is a case of diphtheria? Antitoxin should be used, for it is a specific." What is diphtheria? A toxemic subject with gastro-intestinal catarrh becomes infected from decomposition of animal food eaten in excess of digestive powers. The symptoms are those of tonsilitis, showing a grayish exudite covering the tonsils or other parts of the throat, accompanied by a disagreeable, pungent, fetid breath. There is great prostration. Subjects developing these symptoms have been living haphazardly. Their eating has been too largely of animal foods and starch—the conventional mixtures—and devoid of raw vegetables and fruit. The only animal food may be milk, and the patient a young child. There have been running before, for a longer or shorter term, gastric irritation, constipation, perhaps several gastric attacks—acute indigestion.

In some cases the physical state is so vicious that a severe development of gastro-intestinal putrefaction may end fatally in from one to three days. These are the cases supposed to be overwhelmed by the diphtheritic toxin, which means an acute protein-poisoning—intestinal putrefaction—in a subject already greatly enervated and toxemic.

Malignancy occurs in toxemic subjects who have been carrying continuously a state of gastro-intestinal indigestion from a surfeit of food, in which animal substances, possibly only milk, predominated. The entire organism is more or less infected by the proteid decomposition. A feast-day comes along; an excess produces a crisis; and the organism, which is enervated and toxemic to the point of no resistance, is overwhelmed by septic poisoning.

WHAT CAUSES FATALITY?

Fatal cases in all epidemics are food-drunkards who are very much enervated, toxemic and infected.

It is a crime to feed anything to the sick. No food should be given until all symptoms are gone; then fruit and vegetable juices (never any animal foods—not for weeks). A hot bath should be administered three times daily. Wash out the bowels by enemas every few hours, until all putrescent debris is thoroughly cleared out; and, when possible, give a gastric lavage daily, until the stomach and bowels are thoroughly cleared of all putrescence. The life of the patient depends upon getting rid of the putrid food still remaining in the bowels, before enough putrescence is absorbed to cause death. All epidemic diseases are wholesale food-poisonings among people who are pronouncedly enervated and toxemic. The poisoning by food is on the order of poisoning by chemicals. Those who have least resistance (are most enervated and toxemic) suffer most and succumb the easiest; for the poisoning brings on a crisis of Toxemia, and the two nerve-destroying influences overwhelm the reduced resistance, and may end in death unless wisely treated. All acute diseases are gastro-intestinal infections acting on toxemic subjects. The more enervated and toxemic the subject, the more severe the crisis. Certainly anyone with intelligence should see the danger in giving food when the exciting cause of the disease is food-poisoning.

Keep the patient warm and quiet, and in good air. More treatment is meddlesome. Getting rid of putrefaction is most important. Such diseases develop only in those of pronounced enervation and toxemic, and those of very bad eating habits.

TO SUM UP

To sum up briefly the difference between the toxemic methods and "regular medicine": Toxemia is a system based on the true cause of disease —namely *Toxemia*. Before Toxemia is developed, natural immunization protects from germs, parasites, and all physical vicissitudes.

Toxin is a by-product as constant and necessary as life itself. When the organism is normal, it is produced and eliminated as fast as produced. From the point of production to the point of elim-

ination, it is carried by the blood; hence at no time is the organism free from toxin in the blood. In a normal amount it is gently stimulating; but when the organism is enervated, elimination is checked. Then the amount retained becomes overstimulating—toxic—ranging from a slight excess to an amount so profound as to overwhelm life.

The treatment is so simple that it staggers those who believe in curing. Heroic treatment is disease-building. Find in what way nerve-energy is wasted, and stop it—stop all nerve-leaks. Then returning to normal is a matter of time, in which nature attends to all repairs herself. And she resents help—medical officiousness.

In writing and giving advice, I often make the mistake of taking for granted that the consultant understands what I have in mind. Why should he, when I have not given oral or written expression to my meaning?

In the matter of stopping nerve-leaks, it is easy for me to say: "Find out in what way nerve-energy is wasted, and stop it—stop all nerve-leaks," etc. I am appalled at my stupidity in saying to a patient to stop enervating himself, and allowing the matter to end by naming one or two gross enervating habits; for example: Stop worry; stop smoking; stop stimulants; control your temper; stop eating too rapidly; stop allowing yourself to become excited. Stopping one enervating habit benefits; but dependable health brooks no enervating habits at all.

The Causes of Enervation

TO UNDERSTAND disease, it is necessary to know cause; and, as *Toxemia* is the cause of all diseases, and as enervation—an enervated body and mind—is the cause of *Toxemia*, it behooves those who are sick and want to get well, and who want to know how to stay well, to know what causes enervation.

A normal, healthy person is one who is poised (self-controlled), and who has no nerve-destroying habits. A self-controlled man is a man who is not controlled, kicked, cuffed, or driven by habits.

Man is either the master of himself, or his appetite and sensual pleasures master him. If the former, he enjoys health until worn out; and he should go down at from ninety to one hundred and fifty years of age. If he is inclined to the latter, yet has his habits more or less under control—is moderate—he may live from sixty to ninety years. But if he is a sensualist—is controlled by habits and passions, sits up after bedtime to take a last smoke or eat a lunch, or gets up in the night and smokes (I knew a celebrated physician who used tobacco to secure sleep; he died at fifty-four years of age), or takes a drink to quiet his nerves and make him sleep, or goes the limit venereally—he becomes irritable, grouchy, and dies prematurely.

Excesses transform a man into a disgusting brute. The word "brute" is used here to express the state of one being devoid of self-control. Those of fine constitutions are often converted into neurotics, who have left health and comfort far behind. Many know comfort only for short periods, and then at the instigation of drugs or stimulants.

The youths of our country are fast developing a state of multi-inebriety—jazz, tobacco, alcohol, and petting parties; are developing a sex-neurosis that will be followed by a generation of paralytics, epileptics, insane, morons, idiots, and monstrosities, embracing all who do not die of acute disease.

This class live from thirty until the chloroforming age—sixty years. The majority die early in life. We are fast coming to an age of impotence. I knew one of superior mind who died of ataxia at thirty-five. I quote a few lines from his own writings concerning his state the last year of his life:

Could I but crystallize these midnight tears
  And gather from their beaded bitterness
  A rosary for burning lips to press,
Some pain-born token of these joyless years,
To teach the faith that saves, the hope that cheers;
  Then would I bid these fountains of distress
  Flow fast and free, if their sad floods could bless
Or murmur peace in some poor sufferer's ears.

   .   .   .   .

My world has shrunk at last to this small room,
  Where, like a prisoner, I must now remain.

I'd rather be a captive in the gloom
  Of some damp dungeon, tearing at my chain;
  For then, perchance, my freedom I might gain.
Ah God! to think that I must languish here,
  Fettered by sickness and subdued by pain,
To die a living death from year to year,
Joy banished from my breast and Sorrow brooding there.

    .   .   .   .

I often think how once these stumbling feet,
  That now can scarcely bear me to my bed,
Were swift to follow, as the wind is fleet,
  That baleful beam that to destruction led;

    .   .   .   .

Thou domineering power, or love, or lust,
  Or passion, or whatever else thou art,
How have thy crimson roses turned to dust
  And strewn their withered leaves upon this heart!
Though through my vitals now thy venomed dart
Strikes like an adder's sting, yet still I feel
  From Egypt's flesh-pots it is hard to part;
And my weak, wandering glances often steal
Back to sweet sinful things, until my senses reel.

    .   .   .   .

Still one retreat is left, to which I flee:
Dear dreamy draught, in which I often steep
Body and soul, I turn again to thee,
And drift down Lethe's stream out on Oblivion's sea.

Thirty-five years is a short life for a brain to
live that can conjure the English language as the
above snatches indicate. Thousands pay the price
that this man paid; but very few can win so much
admiration and sympathy with their swan-songs.
Few people can read the psychology of swan-songs.
Often they are an epitome of a lifetime.

ENERVATING HABITS

BABIES

Babies should not be trundled about too much; should not sleep in their mothers' arms; should not be exposed to bright lights, loud talking, noises, too much heat or cold; should not be jolted about in baby-buggies, automobiles, trains, street cars.

The very young are made sick by too much excitement of all kinds. Very young children should be kept quiet enough to favor sleep all the time, except when bathed and when clothes are changed. They should not be taken up every time they do any fretting. All that is needed is to make them dry and change their positions.

Young children should not be fed oftener than every four hours, and not that often unless they are awake. To awaken a child for food is very unnecessary and harmful.

A human being is a cerebro-spinal dynamo, and should be kept as much as possible in a static state, conserving nerve-energy for future use. Poise or self-control—teaching a child to be contented alone—must be started at birth.

Children need no entertainment. When left alone, they find entertainment in becoming acquainted with themselves.

Children that are forced in the matter of being entertained—dancing attendance on them—develop discontent and bring on enervation, which favors "the diseases peculiar to children."

Children of school age are enervated by being urged in school work, exercise, and all kinds of excitement. Play should be limited. When hysteria shows up, stop the play.

With study, examinations, exercise without desire, competitive engagements of all kinds, the craving for food is enormous. But when a growing child is forced to the limit of its nervous capacity, nature must conserve in some way; and as there is no way to sidestep convention's eternal grind, the normal desire for food is lost.

Forced Feeding to Increase Weight.—The whole system of school feeding is one of destroying health by enervating, if not killing, the will.

The federal government is ruining thousands of our young men, teaching them the sick habit. The government should give them a pension and turn them loose. The present coddling is pernicious, not only for the ex-soldier, but also for those who are interested in keeping their hospital jobs.

Doctors must be able to detect cunning and craft. The sick habit often starts as a joke, an experiment—just to see how those interested will take it—and ends in deceiving the deceiver.

A common habit, and one that often leads to a sick habit, is self-pity—being sorry for one's self. Children are inclined to play sick to buy what they want.

Giving even school lunches enervates by building dissatisfaction. It is disease-building. Children must be given an independent spirit—pride will save the world. Then, to add to all this routine of nerve-destroying customs of our schools, teeth must be straightened; which means pressure on nerves and more or less irritation. The tonsils and appendix must be removed. This is a pernicious medical fad. Feed right, and there will be no excuse for operations.

Vaccine and serums must be used to immunize from disease that results from the enervation brought on from all preceding causes. This is another senseless fad.

People are sick from wrong living. Operations remove effects. Stop the cause, and disease goes away. Nature cures, when allowed to do so, by removing the causes of enervation.

Children Pampered and Spoiled.—This brings on the bad and enervating habits of irritability, wilfulness, overeating, improper eating, and temper. Many of the older children use tobacco, coffee, and an excessive amount of sweets and pastry. Self-abuse begins early in many, and is the cause of stomach symptoms. Adolescence comes with excessive dancing, loss of sleep, smoking, drinking, lasciviousness, venereal disease, and the fear springing from the contemplation of the consequences. Irritable children are hard to do anything for. The reason they are irritable is because they are pampered—not made to mind.

It is a crime not to control children. They should be compelled to obey. But do not wait until they are sick. A cranky irritability will help bring on disease and keep a child sick.

Fear.—Fear is the greatest of all causes of enervation. Children are subject to many fears. They are educated to fear the dark, the bogy-man, and punishment. Parents often keep children in a state of fear by irritably cuffing them for the slightest excuse. There are many parents who do their "scrapping" before their children. It is a dreadfully common thing to do.

Outlawry begins at home and at the breast of the mother. A child that cannot respect its parents will not respect the laws of the state or nation. No parent is respected who is not obeyed at once and without capitulation. Unconditional surrender is the discipline necessary for character-building. But children will not obey laws that parents disregard.

In domestic infelicity are born disease and crime, and no amount of doctoring by doctors of medicine, law, and theology can cure; for none of them removes the cause. Those who die of chronic disease have no self-control.

There is much fear and anxiety in a child's life. No child can thrive living in a state of fear in home, school, or church. Discipline taught by respected parents brings love and not fear.

Longevity has increased since hell-fire and brimstone have ceased to be taught and to build fear. A morality kept intact by fear is not health-imparting, and is not a morality at all. Remove the fear, and mob license succeeds it. Fear and love are antidotal. Man has been taught to fear God, and at the same time love Him. Where the fear is real, the love is fictitious. Love being the basis on which ethics is built, a love founded on fear builds humbug ethics; and this is the foundation of all the conventional lies of our civilization.

Fear in all lines concerning children, from their conception to their birth, and on through school life, social life, and marriage, leads to enervation. The dearth of worth-while knowledge of how to feed and otherwise care for children keeps up an unnecessary worry with parents concerning their health. How to teach the young to avoid breaking their health and handicapping their minds by excesses in play, eating, drinking, in controlling temper and emotions, and in self-pollution is a knowledge sadly lacking in nearly all homes. Disease follows these excesses in the young. There is not a habit so self-destructive and so generally practiced as venereal excitement; and there is no habit receiving so little attention from parents.

Ataxia is supposed to be caused by syphilis, but in fact, it is caused by cerebro-spinal enervation, brought on from sensuality in all forms—particularly venereal. Subjects of this disease usually begin onanism early in life. Parents should teach children to avoid destroying habits. I have had locomotor-ataxia cases confess to me that they began their self-pollution as early as eight years of age. Ten to fifteen are the years when active pollution begins. Unless a physician is very tactful, youths will not confess. I will say that very few boys have been untruthful to me. This practice is not quite so common with the opposite sex.

The physical abuse in this line is not nearly so enervating as allowing the mind to dwell on sex-subjects. Lascivious dreaming debauches the victim as much as excessive venery. Early pollution, followed by excessive venery, often commonizes a mind that would shine in the forum and in intellectual pursuits. There is a difference, however, in garrulity and garrulous parroting, and giving a feast of reason. Bright intellects at twenty and twenty-five often degenerate into mediocrity at forty-five because of brain-enervation due to venereal excess. Add to sex-abuse tobacco, coffee, tea, alcohol, and excessive or wrong eating, and no wonder man at sixty is fit for little else than chloroforming, if nature has not already administered euthanasia.

ADULTS

Adults, too, have much fear in their lives. The bread-and-butter problem gives anxiety; but when enough has been accumulated, so that fear along this line is unnecessary, fear is felt that something may happen that will put them back in the bread-line. Why? There is no confidence in business ethics—there is no God in business.

Business Worries.—Business worries are a source of enervation. Business—any business—is not the cause of worry. A work well done is a delight, and anything that delights is character-building. A work slovenly carried on dissatisfies; but the worrier never looks within to find the cause. This life brings enervation in time, and disease as a sequel; then more worries looking for a cure. Business is what a man makes of it. A thorough understanding of business, with honesty and industry, removes all worries and saves nerve-energy. Worry does not build efficiency; neither is inefficiency removed by worrying. Worry, lack of control over the emotions, improper eating, stimulants, all build disease.

Nothing is so conducive to poise as a thorough understanding of one's personal habits and occupation. Bluff and bluster may put the idea of efficiency "across" to the people for a time; but, as surely as chickens come home to roost, the truth will out. Worry, even though presenting a smooth exterior, will break through; the worker will break down—disease will claim him for its own. Housewives who carry a burden of worry become enervated and lose health. The cause of their worry is lack of control in eating, lack of control of the emotions, lack of care of the body, and lack of efficiency. Instead of resolutely going to work to remove all their defects, they are downed by them. An uncontrollable temper must be downed, or it will down the one who gives way to it. Gossip is not an admirable quality, and, unless overcome, it will in time drive friends away. Envy and jealousy are cancers that eat the soul out of those who indulge them. What is left to love when the soul is gone?

When anyone, from indolence and health-destroying habits, allows himself to gravitate below the standard expected of him by his friends, he must not be surprised when they run away from him.

Who are the old people who are left alone? Those who have lived selfish lives—who have demanded entertainment when they should have been entertaining themselves. Happiness and entertainment must come from within—from a love of service, work, and books. If this fountain of youth and pleasure is not found before old age creeps over us, we shall find ourselves alone. Even in the midst of a throng we shall be alone, forever alone. What could be more pathetic?

Self-Indulgence.—Self-indulgence is contrary to ethics and brings its condemnation. What about the ethics of gluttons—what about their religion? Excess in everything follows on the heels of abnormal selfish indulgence. Coming under this head are self-pity and a desire for cure. Extravagant habits, even if there is an inexhaustible supply, builds a self-destructive morale, on the heels of which, like a nemesis, runs the trail to premature death. The causes are called heart disease, apoplexy, paralysis, kidney disease, suicide, etc.;

but what is in a name? Names are all misleading; for the cause—first, last, and all the time—is a selfish body and mind—destructive self-indulgence.

A study of nature reveals the fact that man must live for service; not giving alms, but helping others to help themselves.

Self-indulgence in the use of stimulants, even in moderation, is a constant drain on the nervous system; and a time comes when the last cigar, the last cup of coffee, the last hearty meal, snaps the vital cord; and the contingency is always unexpected and a surprise.

Overwork is said to enervate; but this is an excuse behind which are hidden many bad habits that kill, rather than the work. Work without pleasure in the work is enervating and disease-building; an unsatisfied mind—a desire to engage in some other work before efficiency has been attained in the work engaged in; more desire for pay than to do good work. A work is never well done until it takes on the individuality of the worker. We should work with the creative instinct. Our work should be created in the image of its creator—love of the creator; of the work, not the emoluments.

Dissatisfaction and overworked emotions are enervating. Worry, fear, grief, anger, passion, temper, overjoy, depression, dissatisfaction, self-pity, pride, egotism, envy, jealousy, gossip, lying, dishonesty, failing to meet obligations and appointments, taking advantage of misunderstandings, abusing the credulity of friends, abusing the confidence of those who confide in us—all enervate and in time build incurable disease.

Grief.—Grief is enervating. Those who are very enervated and toxemic will be prostrated by grief, and, unless put to bed and kept warm and quiet, and without food, may die. Food eaten under such circumstances will not digest, but acts as a poison. Some people are made invalids for life by a great grief.

Shock.—Shock, mental or physical, may enervate so greatly as to kill by heart failure, or be followed by permanent nervousness. Wrong eating or overeating may prevent a return to health. The shell-shock that many soldiers suffered during the World War was converted into permanent invalidism by tobacco and other enervating habits. Certainly overeating prevents a return to health.

Anger.—Anger is very enervating. A daily shock of anger will build profound enervation. A temper that flies at the slightest provocation ruins digestion and builds nervousness. Unless controlled, epilepsy may evolve, and cancer may end life. The chronic grouch is liable to build ulcer or cancer of the stomach. Those who cannot control their temper often build rheumatic arthritis, hard arteries, gall-stone, and early old age.

Egotism.—Because of self-love, selfishness, misanthropy, and distrust, the egotist sees unfriendliness in all the acts of others—every hand is against him. This causes enervation and Toxemia, which lead on to many nervous derangements, and even insanity. A misanthrope loves self above everything and everybody. The moment the nearest and dearest friend is suspected, the friend's head comes off figuratively. The egotist hates all who fail to feed his vanity. Hate and anger are always on tap, but draped with a choleric smile when finesse or stratagem demands. Friendship, honor, honesty, and veracity must go when self-love is being impinged upon or neglected. Men of this type have no gratitude. They demand everything, and give nothing without an ulterior motive. Where egotism is mild, it may not go beyond a disagreeable, overbearing selfishness.

Selfishness.—A selfish nature always looks after self first. A common type of selfishness is interpreted as love of children. But when a son or daughter marries against the father's wish, disinheritance follows. Why? Because ambition is piqued. Love is oftener a selfish ambition than affection. Selfishness leads on to enervation and Toxemia.

Ambition.—Ambition of a selfish type brings on ill-health; for it meets with so many disappointments. Where successful, it enables the one who succeeds to gratify his sensual nature, resulting in all the so-called diseases following in the wake of selfish gratification. A *noble ambition* goes with self-control and service to mankind, and health and long life are two of the rewards. Ambition for display, ostentation, gives an evanescent gratification; but it costs more in wasted nerve-energy than it is worth.

Thousands of semi-invalid women bring on toxemic crises as their reward for giving dinners and displaying dress, homes, and furnishings.

Women gratify silly, stupid ambitions, and pay for their thrills in broken health.

Many waste more energy at an afternoon card party than they can renew in a week.

Envy.—Envy of a low and disease-producing type is of a begrudging nature. The man possessing this kind of envy is a vandal. He will slip a monkey-wrench into the machinery of those whom he envies. He will poison reputations by innuendo.

Who steals my purse steals trash; 'tis something, nothing;
'Twas mine, 'tis his, and has been slave to thousands;
But he who filches from me by good name
Robs me of that which not enriches him,
And makes me poor indeed.   (Shakespeare.)

When safe, such a person will go the limit in doing even bodily harm to those whose merits tower over his. Laudable envy is that of a desire to equal in success the one envied. To rejoice in the success of others, and try to equal them, where the success has been achieved on merit, builds a healthy mind and body.

Love and Jealousy.—According to Solomon: "Love is strong as death; jealousy is cruel as the grave." Solomon should have known.

Shakespeare knew about everything worth knowing up to his time. He said:

> How many fools serve maddened jealousy!
> The venomed clamors of a jealous woman
> Poison more deadly than a mad dog's tooth.

The systematic poisoning of overwrought emotions has been known since reasoning began; but, aside from knowing that "a poison is generated in the system" from great anger, love, jealousy, hate, and grief, just what the poison is, and the *modus operandi* of its production, have never been satisfactorily explained until made clear by the Philosophy of Toxemia. The pathology of jealousy Shakespeare knew well, as evidenced by the words he put into the mouths of some of his characters.

Excessive emotion—jealousy, for example, or great anger—precipitates a profound enervation, which inhibits elimination. This floods the blood with toxin, and brings on a malignant Toxemia in the form of toxin drunkenness, which in people of a belligerent nature causes them *to run amuck*. Murder, several murders, are sometimes committed. In those with more consideration for others—those with less self-love—suicide ends the psychological storm.

Jealousy and unrequited love, when not malignant—developing in a vicious, unmoral subject—

in time undermine the constitution by keeping up a gradually increasing state of enervation and Toxemia. Catarrhal inflammations and ulcerations get better and worse, with no hope of final recovery until the causes of enervation are overcome —namely, enervating habits of mind and body, of which jealousy is chief.

Overeating.—Overeating is a common and universal enervating habit; eating too much fat—cream, butter, fat meats, oils, rich pastries, sweets; eating too often; eating between meals, and checking digestion with water-drinking between meals.

Food-inebriety is more common than alcholinebriety. The subconscious is as busy as a hive of bees in substituting, antidoting, and reparation work; substituting one stimulating excess for another—demanding whisky, tobacco, opium, etc., for gluttonous eating; thrills, shocks, sensual excesses for food-poisoning. Ungratified sense-demands are appeased by food excesses or other stimulants; and when nature is balked in her demands, the victim runs amuck.

A French sheep-herder's daughter, being opposed by her father in marrying a lover, killed the parent while he slept by their campfire. A short time after the tragedy some men came upon the camp and discovered the girl eating her father's heart, which she had cut out and roasted in the fire. When surprised at her cannibalistic feast, she held up what was left of the heart, and, with a sardonic laugh, declared: "He broke my heart, and I am eating his."

Only a short time ago the overwrought nerves of a jazz- and alcohol-crazed girl forced her to kill her mother because the latter undertook to oppose her in the gratification of her subconscious demands for more stimulation.

When enervation and Toxemia have reached the stage of inebriety seen in the two girls mentioned above, civil and moral laws have abdicated to the subconscious laws, which, like cosmic law and order, are unmoral, but run true to necessity.

Psychological, like physical, cyclones are out of the regular order; yet they are obeying the laws of their nature. They have no scruples to gainsay, but tear through order as ruthlessly as fiends.

Every human being should know that such phenomena are potential to him, and that the road to such catastrophes in enervating habits.

Prohibition is a beautiful ideal, but it is palliating one social disease while it is building a greater.

What mother would not rather have her son brought home from the corner grog-shop drunk than see him escorted to jail hand-cuffed to an officer?

Enervation and Toxemia focused on the brain bring out neurotic states, with all kinds of symptom-complexes. Drunkenness substitutes for bank robbery and other outlawry. So long as food-drunkenness retains its prestige with the professions—prescribed by doctors; babbled to us Sundays, and deciding our brawls on Monday—it will take more than statutes to force law and order. Most of our laws are made while the law-makers are drunk on food and tobacco.

Drunkenness and crime of all kinds are vicarious toxin eliminations—crises of Toxemia. Enforcing temperance and control of crime must fail in its object—namely, causing people to be temperate and law-abiding. The reason should be obvious to the student of nature. Our wants are based on our subconscious needs; sentiment and ethics have nothing to do with it. Our subconscious is not moral nor immoral; it belongs to the Great Cosmos, which is systematic, perfect in order, but unmoral. Intemperance of any kind establishes a want which, if not satisfied in the usual way, will turn to other ways of being satisfied. The surgeon, laws, and anodynes perhaps relieve effects, but cures are based on removing causes. Legislatures are quack doctors. Self-control is the only cure. To develop self-control, the need must be understood.

The gluttonous build putrefaction in the bowels. Nerve-energy is used up in resisting systemic infection. The supply of blood to the surface of the body for purposes of warmth—radiation—resisting cold and heat, is called to the mucous membrane of the gastro-intestinal canal to neutralize the septic material that is about to enter the system through the absorbents. The mucous membrane becomes turgid with blood, establishing a mucorrhea (excessive secretion of mucous.) This is what we call catarrh. This secretion mechanically obstructs absorption of putrescence, and also antidotes the poison by bringing the antibodies from the blood.

A battle-royal is on all the time in the intestines of the gluttonous. The subconscious musters all the help possible, and when the system is drained of autogenerated antidotes, the victim is sent by his subconscious to find alcohol, tobacco, coffee, tea, condiments, and more food. Moral preachments, and prohibitory laws passed by Solons drunk on toxin, bowel putresence, and tobacco, like all monstrosities, are abortions.

Insatiable desire for food and stimulants means an enervated state of the body brought on from overindulgence—overstimulation.

A driving desire for food three times a day means enervation; trouble is only a little farther on. The wise will get busy and correct appetites.

Perverted appetites are built by overeating; eating rich food until enjoyment is lost for staple or plain foods; excessive use of stimulants—alcohol, tobacco, coffee, tea; excessive use of butter, salt, pepper, and rich dressings; eating without a real hunger (real hunger will take the plainest foods with a relish); eating when sick or uncomfortable; eating at off hours, between meals; eating until uncomfortable.

Gossips are always slanderers, and slanderers are always and forever potential liars. If they do not know that they are broadcasting lies, they are criminally careless in not endeavoring to find whether the tale they gossip is true or not. *Gossip enervates the gossiper.*

Gossips are always enervated; for they live in fear of being discovered. Their secretions are always acid. They are inclined to develop pyorrhea and mucous-membrane infections. They are slow to recover from catarrhal crises of Toxemia.

Gossips are empty-headed slaves to their habits of slander and spite; they are malignant parasites that feed upon carrion. They are the lowest type of criminals; hell-monsters that kill with their breath. They often die of cancer.

Sycophancy.—Flatterers look like friends, as wolves like dogs. (Byron.) He hurts me most who lavishly commends. (Churchill.)

A real sycophant, like all people who are not honest, lives a life that enervates, and which nature condemns early.

Dishonesty. — Dishonesty eventually hardens the arteries, and cancer ends a miserable existence.

Retrospection

MORE might have been said, and no doubt better said, about how we human beings vandalize our minds and bodies; but enough has been told for open-minded people to see that the only nemesis on our heels is our habits. O. W. Holmes, in his "The Autocrat of the Breakfast Table," had this to say concerning habit:

> Habit is the approximation of the animal system to the organic. It is a confession of failure in the highest function of being, which involves a perpetual self-determination, in full view of all existing circumstances.

Autonomy or self-government is met at the threshold of life by all the conventional superstitions, and educated into a lot of habits, such as curing without removing cause. This, combined with man's inclination to hedonism (the doctrine that pleasure is the only good), leads to a life of failure, in spite of man's potential desire to rise above the forces that hold him down. "Toxemia Explained" will help all who study it carefully to understand what disease is, and how it is brought on. This knowledge will help the wise and self-controlled to sidestep disease, and the medical octopus that unwittingly vandalizes the sick.

The profession is made up of an army of educated men; and I believe the majority are gentlemen, and are endeavoring to serve humanity. Education and ethics, when established on fallacy and given the prestige of numbers—given an overwhelming majority—can make the fallacy true, so far as the herd is concerned.

All I ask of laymen or the profession is honestly to put my philosophy to the acid test. Yes, prove, if possible, that I am mistaken, and then give me what is coming to me!

Man makes his own diseases. This book tells how he does it. And he is the one who can bring health back. He and his subconsciousness alone can cure. Doctors cannot cure. Only very rarely is surgical vandalism a *dernier resort*, unless bad treatment forces unnecessary emergencies.

> The body is strong or weak, as the case may be, depending entirely on whether the nerve-energy is strong or weak. And it should be remembered that the functions of the body are carried on well or badly according to the amount of energy generated.

A Few Suggestions

THE following suggestions may be of assistance to those who wish to maintain their present state of good health, or help them to bring themselves from their present state of impaired health to that of good health. Those who are badly handicapped, and who wish more detailed information, will have to have the advice fitted to their particular cases through individual instructions.

The first thing on awaking in the morning, the Tilden system of tensing exercises should be practiced for from fifteen to thirty minutes. (See exercises at the end of this chapter.) Following the exercise, go to the bathroom and, while standing in warm water, take a quick, warm sponge-bath. Then follow this with plenty of dry-towel or friction-mitten rubbing. At night, before retiring, give the body a thorough friction rubbing again. If not convenient to take the warm sponge-bath in the morning, use the dry rub in the morning and the warm sponge-bath at night before retiring.

Eat three meals a day and no more; no eating nor drinking between meals. Use the following rules to guide you in "when to eat, when not to eat, and how to eat":

Rule No. 1.—Never eat unless you have been absolutely comfortable in mind and body from the previous mealtime.

Rule No. 2.—Thoroughly masticate and insalivate every mouthful of starchy food, and give the rest of your food plenty of attention.

Rule No. 3.—Never eat without a keen relish.

If the bowels do not move during the day, before retiring at night use a small enema—a pint of warm water. Put it into the bowels, and allow it to remain for five to ten minutes; then solicit a movement. Proper mastication, right combinations of food, and plenty of tensing exercise to the abdomen will bring about proper bowel action.

As to what to eat—For those in ordinarily good health the following rules will serve as a guide:

Fruit Breakfast		Starch Breakfast
Starch Lunch	or	Fruit Lunch
Regulation Dinner		Regulation Dinner

The regulation dinner may be taken at noon in place of the lunch, if it is more convenient.

Fruit Breakfast.—Any kind of fresh fruit or berries followed with either milk, fifty-fifty (half warm milk and half hot water), or teakettle tea (hot water with two or three tablespoonfuls of cream to the cup).

Starch Breakfast.—Toast, Shredded Wheat, Triscuit, Rye Crisp, well-baked muffins, corn bread or biscuit, griddle-cakes, waffles, cooked cereal (any one of foregoing), followed with fresh or cooked fruit, without sugar. The dry starches should be eaten with a little butter, and not soaked up with milk or cream. This insures thorough mastication. The cereals should be taken with a little cream and salt—no milk or sugar. The griddle-cakes and waffles may be accompanied with honey and butter, followed with teakettle tea.

If desired, the starch breakfast may be followed with fresh fruit instead of a beverage.

Starch Lunch.—The same as the starch breakfast. Occasionally a piece of plain cake and ice-cream.

Fruit Lunch.—The same as the fruit breakfast. Occasionally a piece of fruit pie and a piece of cheese, or some form of desert, followed with fresh fruit.

Regulation Dinner.—No. 1: Meat, two cooked non-starchy vegetables, and a combination salad.

No. 2: Starch, two cooked non-starchy vegetables, and a combination salad.

Meat: Any kind of fresh meat, cheese, nuts, eggs, bacon, fish, or fowl.

Starch: Potatoes (sweet or Irish), macaroni, rice, Hubbard squash, dry beans and peas, tapioca, pumpkin, or any of the starches listed above.

Cooked Non-starchy Vegetables: Beets, carrots, parsnips, cabbage, lettuce, cauliflower, Brussels sprouts, green corn, green beans and peas, asparagus, onions, eggplant, salsify, tomatoes, cucumbers, celery, spinach, greens, summer squash, etc.

Combination Tilden Salad: Lettuce, tomatoes, and cucumber; lettuce, celery, and apple; lettuce, apple, and orange, or any other fruit. Dress with salt, oil, and lemon juice.

Regulation Dinner No. 1 should be taken every other day, and Dinner No. 2 the alternate days.

Of course, there are many variations and additions to the above suggestions, but details cannot be gone into in this book. Those who wish to have more detailed suggestions should read the monthly periodical, *Dr. Tilden's Health Review and Critique,* and his *Cook Book.*

DR. TILDEN'S TENSING EXERCISES

Begin by tensing the leg muscles from the toes to the body, as follows: First extend the toes as far as you can; then grip, as it were, by forcing the toes forward toward the heels, and at the same time make the muscles of the legs hard to the body. Completely relax. Do not repeat the tension again until the muscles are soft; then tense again, repeating the contraction and extension.

Tense the hands and arms in the same way. Extend the fingers as far as possible, making the muscles hard to the shoulders; then grip the fingers and shut the fist, hardening the muscles to the shoulders. Do this five times; then tense the legs five times; then the hands and arms again.

Fold a pillow and put under the shoulders, so that when the head drops back it will not touch anything. Lift the head forward, the chin to the chest; drop the head back again as far as it will go; then lift. Do this four or five times. Then, with the pillow still under the shoulders, lock the fingers under the head, allowing the head to rest in the hands. Swing the head from side to side, up and down, and rotate, carrying each movement as far as possible.

Then push the folded pillow down under the hips and go through the leg movements of riding a bicycle. Then, with legs extended in the air, move each leg from side to side, allowing one to pass the other, scissor-fashion; changing, however, each time they pass, having first one leg forward and then the other.

Tense the abdomen, making the muscles as hard as possible, and at the same time kneading the muscles with the hands. This exercise is necessary for overcoming constipation. In women, the uterine ligaments will be strengthened, lifting and overcoming falling and misplaced positions of the womb. The muscles of the bladder and rectum will be improved by these exercises. Piles— prolapsus of the rectal mucous membrane—will be overcome. An irritable bladder and prostate enlargments will be benefited by these exercises.

Then sit up and turn the face to the right as far as possible; then to the left as far as possible; then allow the head to drop over, so as to bring the ear close to the shoulder, and then carry it over to the opposite shoulder.

These movements of the head and neck are necessary to remove deposits that take place between the vertebræ, and in grooves and openings in bones where the nerves and arteries pass. If the hearing is bad, these movements will improve it. If the sense of smell is not so acute as it should be, by keeping up the exercises the olfactory nerve will be freed and the power of smell will be improved. The taste, too, will be bettered. All the nerves of special sense will be invigorated. The pneumogastric nerve and all the vital nerves controlling vital organs are invigorated by this exercise. When nerves are pressed upon by organic deposits, the movements above described will cause the deposits to be absorbed. The muscles of the neck will develop; the muscles of the face will develop; one will grow to look and feel younger.

These exercises must be gone through with, not only before getting up, but every three or four hours during the day. You may think that this is very laborious, but it is the price you must pay to get well. So begin at once, and be faithful!

Sit on the edge of the bed, and sway the body from side to side as far as possible; then follow with a twisting movement, attempting to look behind over the shoulders. Sit up in bed, and sway backward and forward, compelling the spine to bend from the small of the back up to the head, forward and backward. This loosens up the spine and invigorates the nerves that are sent off to the lower part of the body.

Get on the knees and elbows; then push the body forward as far as possible without falling upon the abdomen; then push back as far as possible. Go back and forth, while in this position, until tired; then drop on either the left or right shoulder while the hips are highly elevated. This is called the knee-shoulder position. The knee and elbow position, with the movements described, I call the "Irish Mail movements." It is necessary to practice both these movements and positions in overcoming constipation, prolapsus of the bowels, rectum, or womb, and piles.

Place the forefingers over the closed eyes, and rub gently from side to side. Then remove the fingers and rotate the eyeballs, reversing the movement to relieve the tire. Place the forefingers on the wings of the nose; press together and move from side to side. When the weather is nice, it is well to walk in the open air as often as possible.

INDEX

A

Acute disease, cannot manifest without preparation, 27.
Acute malignancy, defined, 99.
Adults, fear in, 110.
Alcohol, use of, 103, 110, 121.
Ambition, selfish, enervating, 115.
Anemia, pernicious, 22.
    blood transfusion for, 78.
Anger, enervating, 113, 114.
"Anonymous," quotations from, 42.
Antitoxin, 97.
    in diphtheria, 98.
Apoplexy, 33, 54.
Appendix, removal of, 107.
Arteries, hardening of, 54.
Asthma, 67.
Ataxia, locomotor, 103, 109.
Athletes, die early, 84.
Autogenerated poison, cause of disease, 26, 57.
Auto-immunization, 91.

B

Babies, habits in, 105.
Bathing, proper, 125.
Blood, ruptured vessel, 33.
    amount of toxin in varies, 72,
    transfusion in pernicious anemia, 78.
    degeneration of vessels, 84.
    state of, makes disease possible, 79, 92.
    toxin carried by, 101.
Bowels, derangement of, 91.
    attention to, 96, 99, 126.
Brain, hemorrhage in, 33.

Bright's disease, once innocent cold, 52.
Bronchitis, 92.
Business worry, 111.

C

Cabot, Dr., on diagnosis, 19.
Cancer, how built, 12, 22, 23, 35, 60.
    once innocent cold, 52.
    cause of, 53, 60.
Care, in case of megrime, 47.
    of acute diseases, 53.
    of patients, 61, 67, 99.
    of children, 80, 96, 105.
    of muscle fatigue, 88.
Catarrh, 12, 22, 34, 53, 67.
Catching cold habit, 69.
Cause, of disease, 10, 15, 18, 23, 26, 27, 28, 54, 72, 79, 91, 97, 100, 102.
    must be found, 16, 19, 96.
    is constant, 22.
    true, 26.
    of autogenerated poison, 26.
    medley of guesswork, 31.
    serum as, 62.
    of enervation, 102.
Children, our duty toward, 61.
    diseases peculiar to, 64.
    must be kept busy, 81.
    fever in, 96.
    not sick unless toxemic, 97.
    enervating habits in, 105, 106.
    pampered, 107.
Clothes and cleanliness, 58.
Coffee headache, 15.
Cold feet, detrimental, 64.

Colds, at first functional, 23.
    defined, 67.
    catching habit, 69.
Colonitis, a toxemic crisis, 92.
Complexes of symptoms, disease, 52.
Conservation of nerve energy, greatest therapeutic measure, 66.
Constipation, 57, 86.
Contentment, necessary, 80.
Convulsions, 90.
Crises of Toxemia, is disease, 10, 49, 67, 68, 69, 70, 92, 95, 120.
Croup, 67.
Cure, man looking for, 9.
    there is none, 10, 86, 95.
    by diet, 11.
    depends on r e m o v a l of cause, 16.
    what is it, 18, 38, 44.
    medley of guesswork, 31.
    doctors do not, 50.
    all acute diseases can receive, 52.
    product of civilization, 59.
    a delusion, 97.
Cystitis, 68, 90.

D

Deadly germ, 58.
Deficiency diseases, 13.
Diagnosis, Mackenzie, on, 19.
    Cabot, on, 19.
    what is it, 20.
    medical delusion, 93.
Diagnostitians perplexed, 36.
Diets, too many, 9, 11.
Diphtheria, 96.
    antitoxin in, 98.
Disease, cause of, 10, 15, 18, 23, 26, 27, 28, 54, 72, 79, 91, 97, 100, 102.
    cure of, 10, 11, 16, 17, 31, 38, 44, 49, 52, 59, 86, 95, 97.
    man's own building, 9, 11.

Disease—*Continued*
    toxemic crisis, 10, 49, 50, 67, 68, 69, 70, 92, 95, 120.
    organic, cause of, 10, 20, 70.
    Tilden system covers all, 11.
    a common expression of universal enervation, 12.
    deficiency, 13.
    early stages of organic, 22.
    perverted health, 23.
    not an entity, 29, 31, 33, 38, 69.
    extraneous influence n o t cause of, 30.
    made manifest by symptoms, 33.
    what is, 35, 84.
    and symptoms confounded, 36.
    Mackenzie on, 36.
    nature's housecleaning, 49.
    all, once innocent, 52.
    unity of, 60, 70.
    germs as cause of, 61.
    peculiar to children, 64.
    acute, 100.
    in children, 107.
Dishonesty, enervating, 122.
Doctor, man his own, 9.
    cannot cure anything, 50, 87, 124.
    duty of, 51.
Dropsy, 87.
Drug habit, 14.
Drugs, venereal disease curable without, 14.
    and medical science, 30.
    check elimination, 48, 49.

E

Eating, excessive, 69.
    wrong, effect of, 79.
    three meals only, 125.
Effects, only change, 21.
    not cause have been studied, 32.

Egotism, enervating, 114.
Eliminant, most powerful, 9.
Elimination, checked, toxin accumulates, 15, 26, 117.
    checked by drugs, 48.
    vicarious, disease, 49, 67, 102.
    faulty, effect of, 60, 69, 71, 79.
    of waste products of tissue building, 63.
Emotion, excessive, 117.
Enema, use of, 96, 99, 126.
Energy, nerve, waste of, 15, 64.
    normal, effect of, 27.
    controls bodily strength, 63.
    importance of, 63.
    conservation of, 66.
Enervating habits, if continued, build disease, 10, 11, 69.
    must be removed, 15, 95.
    what are they, 105.
    in children, 105.
Enervation, cause of, 15, 17, 102.
    not general cause of disease, 26.
    effect of, 27, 52, 65, 69, 91.
    cause, and not disease, 67.
    general, 71.
    prevents elimination of infection, 78.
Entity, disease not an, 29, 31, 33, 38, 69.
Envy, enervating, 112, 116.
Epidemics, 97, 99.
Epilepsy, 21.
Etiology, truthful, 24.
Exercise, excessive, harmful, 83.
    tensing, 125, 128.
Excessive, venery, enervating, 15.
    eating, 69.
    exercise, harmful, 83.
Extraneous influence, not cause of disease, 30.

F

Facts, without ideas, 16.
Fast, most powerful eliminant, 61.
    fear of, 95.
Fatality, what causes, 99.
Fear, prevents elimination, 49.
    effect of, 79, 90.
    in children, 108.
    in adults, 110.
Feet, cold, harmful, 64.
Fever, septic, cause of, 77.
    scarlet, 96.
Focal infection, 62, 93.
Food, in intestines, on outside of body, 57.
    poisoning, 57, 99.
    proper for children, 97.
    effect of wrong, 79.
    drunkards produce fatal cases, 99.
    for sick, 99.
    for young children, 105.
    inebriety, enervating, 118.
    driving desire for, 120.
    when to take, 125.
Forced feeding increases weight, 106.
Functional derangement precedes structural change, 71.

G

Gall-bladder, stone in, 54, 66.
Gastric lavage, use of, 99.
Gastritis, early stages of, 22, 35, 92.
Germs, accidental, 23.
    as cause of fermentation, 32.
    and disease, 37.
    deadly, 58.
    as cause of disease, 61, 76.
    Toxemia accepts, 62.
Gland impotency, 78.
Goiter, 90.
Gossip enervating, 121.
Grief enervating, 114.

Meningitis, 96.
Metabolism, toxin, waste prod-
cut of, 27.
　　Toxin, a product of, 63, 71,
　　76, 100.
Moderation, what is it, 91.
Muscle fatigue, 88.

N

Nature needs no remedy, 60.
　　effect of interfering with,
　　76.
　　cures when so allowed, 107.
Nerve energy, waste of, 15, 63.
　　normal, effect of, 27.
　　controls bodily strength, 63.
　　importance of, 63, 100.
　　conservation of necessary,
　　66.
Nerve leaks, must be stopped,
101.
Nerves, impinged, 30.
Neuralgia, 88.
Neuritis, 88.
Neurosis, 86.

O

Occupational diseases, 90.
Operation, for tumors, stone,
ulcers, 12.
　　no excuse for, 107.
Organic disease, cause of, 10,
20, 70.
　　early stages of, 22.
Osler, opinion of, 42.
Overeating, is overstimulating,
15.
　　is enervating, 118.
Overwork, does not enervate,
113.

P

Pain, usually first symptom, 34,
36.
Palliatives, are they ever necessary, 14.
　　most cures are, 95.

Paralysis, 34.
　　infantile, 96.
Pathology, study of, 20, 23, 52.
　　of jealousy, 117.
Perfect health, how to establish,
15.
Pernicious anemia, 22.
　　blood transfusions for, 78.
Pharyngitis, 67.
Piles, 88.
Pneumonia, 67, 92.
　　fatality of, 49.
Poise, defined, 80.
　　lack of, 84, 88, 90.
　　necessary, 102, 111.
Poison, disease indirectly due to,
26.
　　per se, not disease, 26, 92.
　　auto-generated, 26, 57.
　　ptomaine, 57.
Preface, 9.
Prevention, what is it, 18.
Prohibition, a beautiful idea,
119.
Protein infection, 22.
Psychological cyclones, 119.
Psychologists, work of, 30, 81.
Ptomaine poisoning, 57.

Q

Quiet, necessary during sickness, 51, 97, 100.
　　necessary in children, 105.

R

Remedy, for tobacco heart, 10.
　　nature needs no, 60.
Regular medicine and Tilden
Philosophy compared, 100.
Rest, necessary for cure, 11, 61,
66.
Retrospection, 123.
Rheumatism, cure of, 11.
　　cause of, 27, 88.
　　an effect, 93.
Roosevelt, cause of death of, 77.

Rules, my principle, 125.
Rush, Benjamin, thought from, 39.

S

Scarlet fever, 96.
Scientific tests, 44.
Secretions of body, overcomes germs, 59.
Self abuse, in children, 107.
Self control brings best in life, 88, 90, 120.
Self indulgence, 112.
Self pity, disease building, 85.
Selfishness, enervating, 115.
Septic fever, cause of, 77.
Septic poisoning, 57.
     following vaccination, 76.
Serums, in children, 105.
Shock, enervating, 114.
Sick habit, 85, 106.
Sinus, infected, 94.
Sleep, unnatural, 85.
Smallpox, cure or prevention of, 16.
Smoking must be overcome, 101.
Spencer, Herbert, on vaccination, 73.
Stimulants, subtilely undermining, 14.
     remove awareness, 15.
     continued use of, 76.
Stone in gall bladder, 54, 66.
Subconscious, influence of, 87.
     not moral nor immoral, 120.
     alone, can cure, 124.
Suggestions, a few, 125.
Summing up, 100.
Surgery, world needs science of, 13.
     unnecessary, 13.
Sycophancy enervates, 122.
Symptomatologly, value of, 33.

Symptoms, hold secret of cause, 20.
     Sir James Mackenzie on, 20, 33.
     a chain of, 34.
     and disease confounded, 36.
     pain, first, 34, 36.
     complex of, signifies crises of Toxemia, 49, 50, 67.
     all have same origin, 53.
     vary, 68.
Syphilis, curable without drugs, 14.
     one cause of, 60.
     in toxemic subjects, 79.
     presence of, 87.

T

Teeth, infected, cause of, 93.
Temper, must be controlled, 101.
Tensing exercise, beneficial, 125.
     explained, 128.
Tension, must be overcome, 85, 90.
     cause of, 90.
Tests, scientific, 44.
Tilden meals, 125.
Tilden system applies to all disease, 11.
Tissue, worn out must be removed, 63, 88.
Tobacco, use of, 47, 103, 107, 110, 113, 114, 121.
Tobacco heart, remedy for, 10.
Tonsilitis, 67, 92, 98.
Tonsils must not be removed, 107.
Toxemia, cause of, must be removed, 10.
     introduction to subject of, 17.
     primary cause of all disease, 18, 23, 26, 27, 72, 79, 91, 97, 100, 102.
     explained, 29, 67.
     crises of, disease, 10, 49, 67, 69, 92, 95, 120.

Toxemia—*Continued*
    defined, 57, 67.
    accepts germ, 62.
    simplifies understanding of
        disease, 96.
Toxemic crises is disease, 10,
    67, 69.
    philosophy f o u n d e d on
        truth, 53.
Toxin, must be eliminated, 11.
    product of metabolism, 63,
        71, 76, 100.
    amount in blood varies, 72.
    a stimulant, 76, 101.
    normal product, 92.
Treatment, proper, 49, 61, 78,
    89, 99.
    for megrime, 47.
    must vary, 68.
    of tense muscles, 90.
    of children, 96.
Truth, as famous men see it, 38.
Tuberculosis, once innocent cold,
    52.
    one cause of, 60.
Tumors, 60.
Typhoid fever, 49.

U

Ulcer of stomach, 12, 21, 35, 52.
    a symptom, 35.
Universal law rules in health
    and disease, 11.
Unnecessary surgery, 13.
Urine, albumin in, 87.

V

Vaccination, Herbert Spencer,
    on, 73.
Vaccines, 57.
    made from products of dis-
        ease, 18.

Vaccines—*Continued*
    are poisons, 72.
    effect of, 76.
    use of in children, 107.
Venereal disease, can be cured
    without drugs, 14.
    fostered by clothes, 58.
Venereal excitement, effect of,
    109.
Vicarious elimination, disease,
    49, 67, 102.

W

Warmth, bodily, necessary, 65,
    100.
Weight, forced feeding increases,
    106.
Womb, tumor in, 90.
Women, painful menstruation
    in, 21.
    megrime in, 47.
    self sacrificing, 86.
    worry in, 111.
Work, sometimes enervating, 66.
    brings contentment, 80.
World needs science of surgery,
    13.
Worry, its connection with dis-
    ease, 40, 68.
    must be overcome, 101.
    business, 111.
Wound, suppurating, 57.

Y

Young children, proper care of,
    105.
Youth, desires speed, 83.
    developing multi-inebriety,
        103.
    fountain of, 112.